Synecdotal Synergy

Coloring Book

By Hafapea

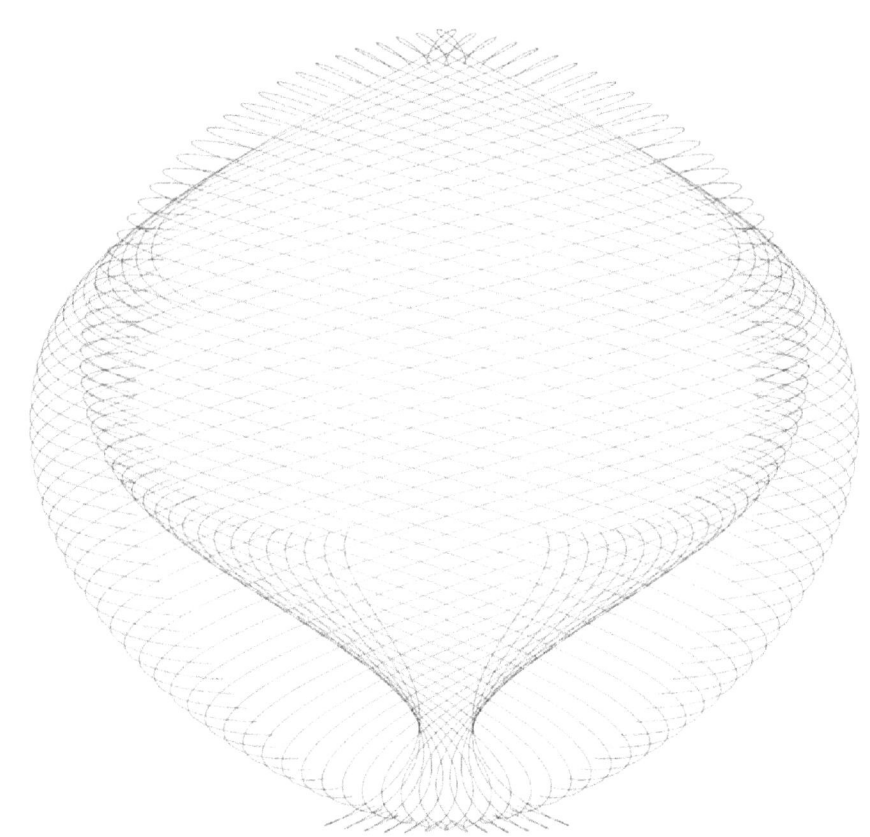

Color your way to happiness.

Synecdotal Synergy Coloring Book
Copyright ©2016 Lisa Mayette, aka Hafapea

Published by Amazon via Createspace.

ISBN-13: 978-1530969975
ISBN-10: 1530969972

Also available:

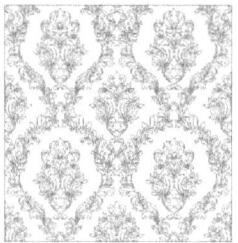

Persnickety Patterns Coloring Book

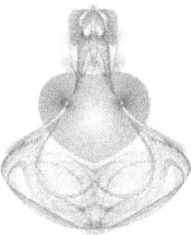

Fractals & Flames Coloring Book

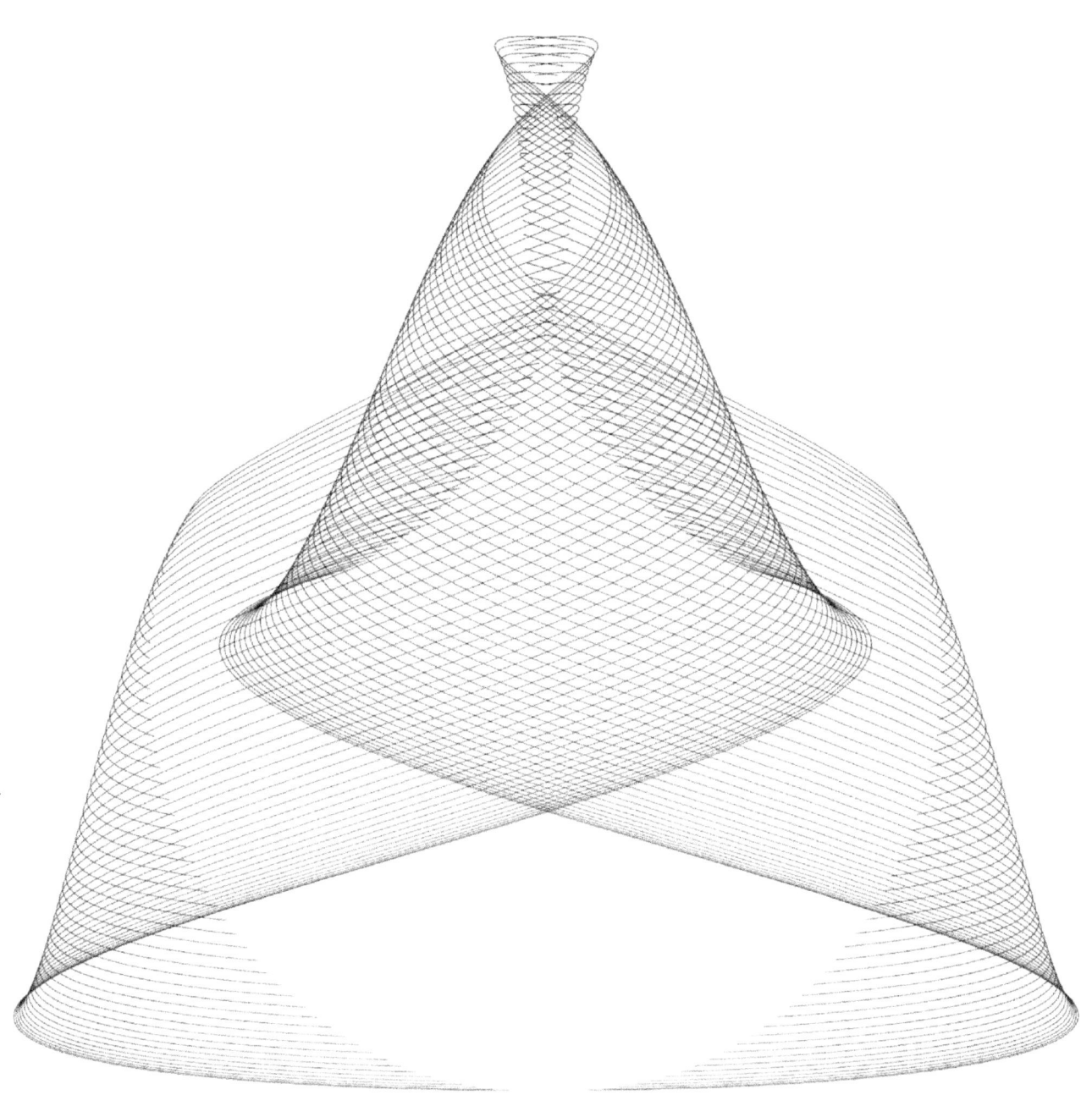

It is not how much we have,
but how much we enjoy, that makes happiness.
Charles Spurgeon

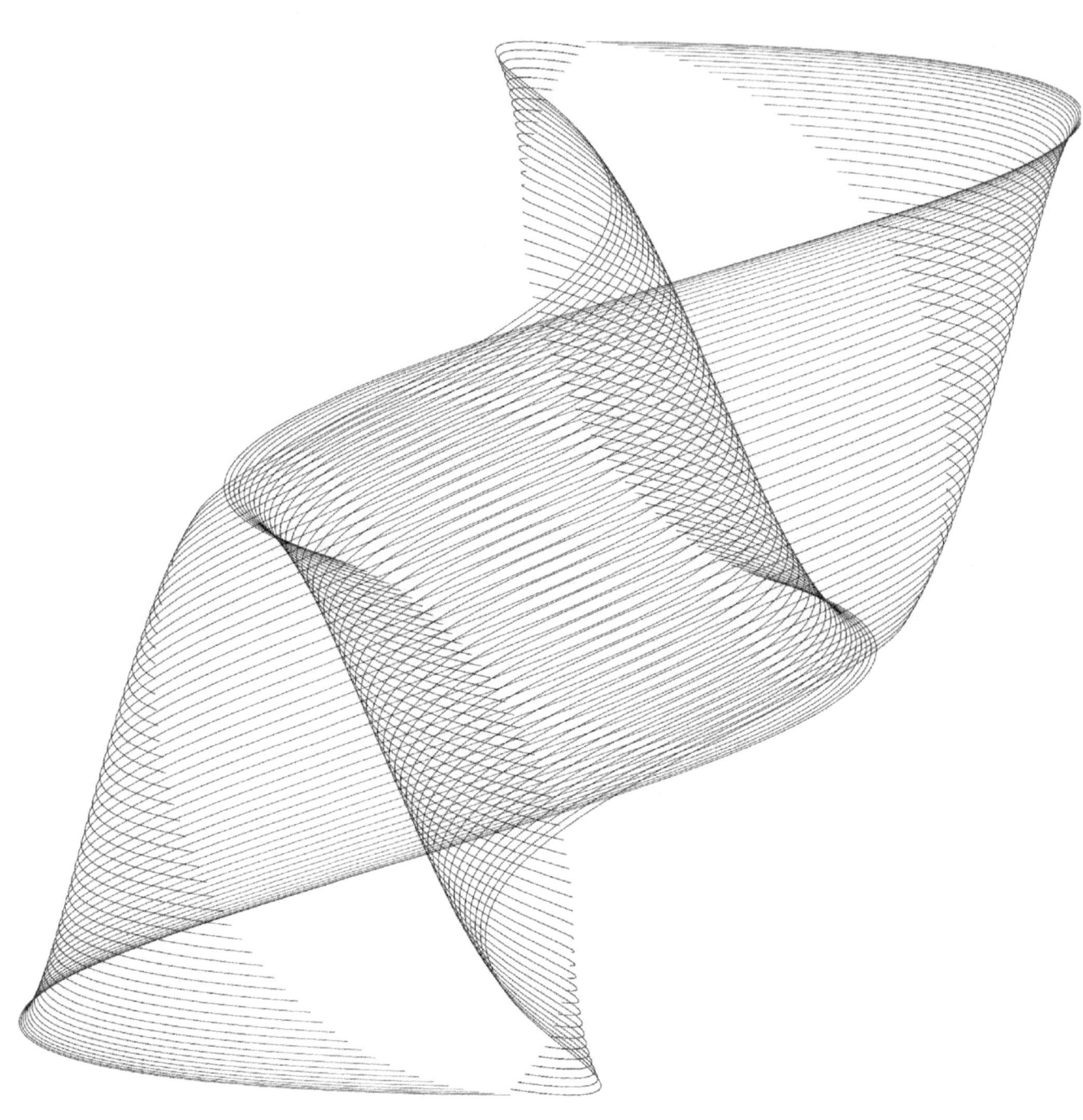

Happiness is when what you think,
what you say, and what you do are in harmony.
Mahatma Gandhi

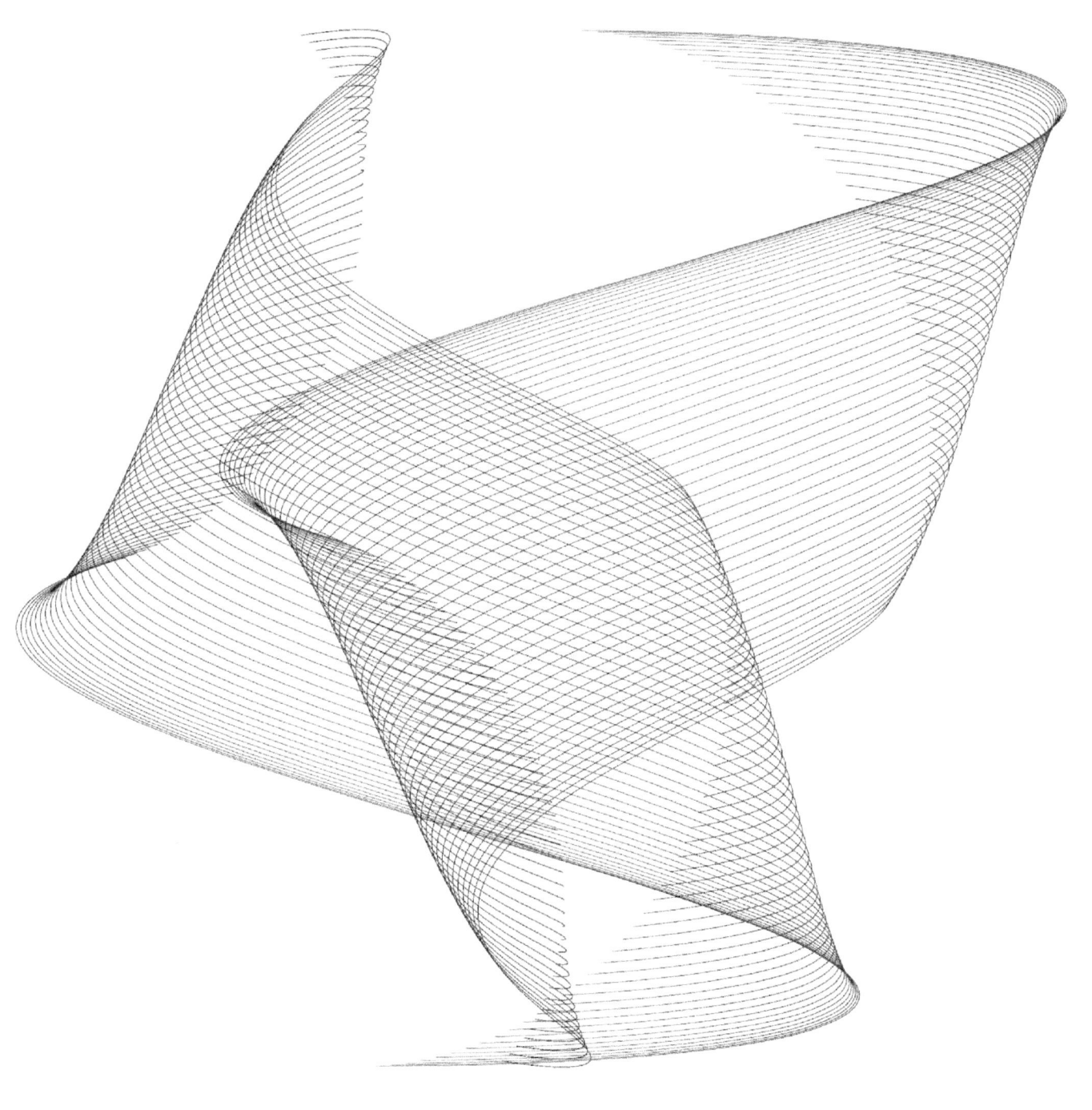

Happiness is not a matter of intensity
but of balance, order, rhythm and harmony.
Thomas Merton

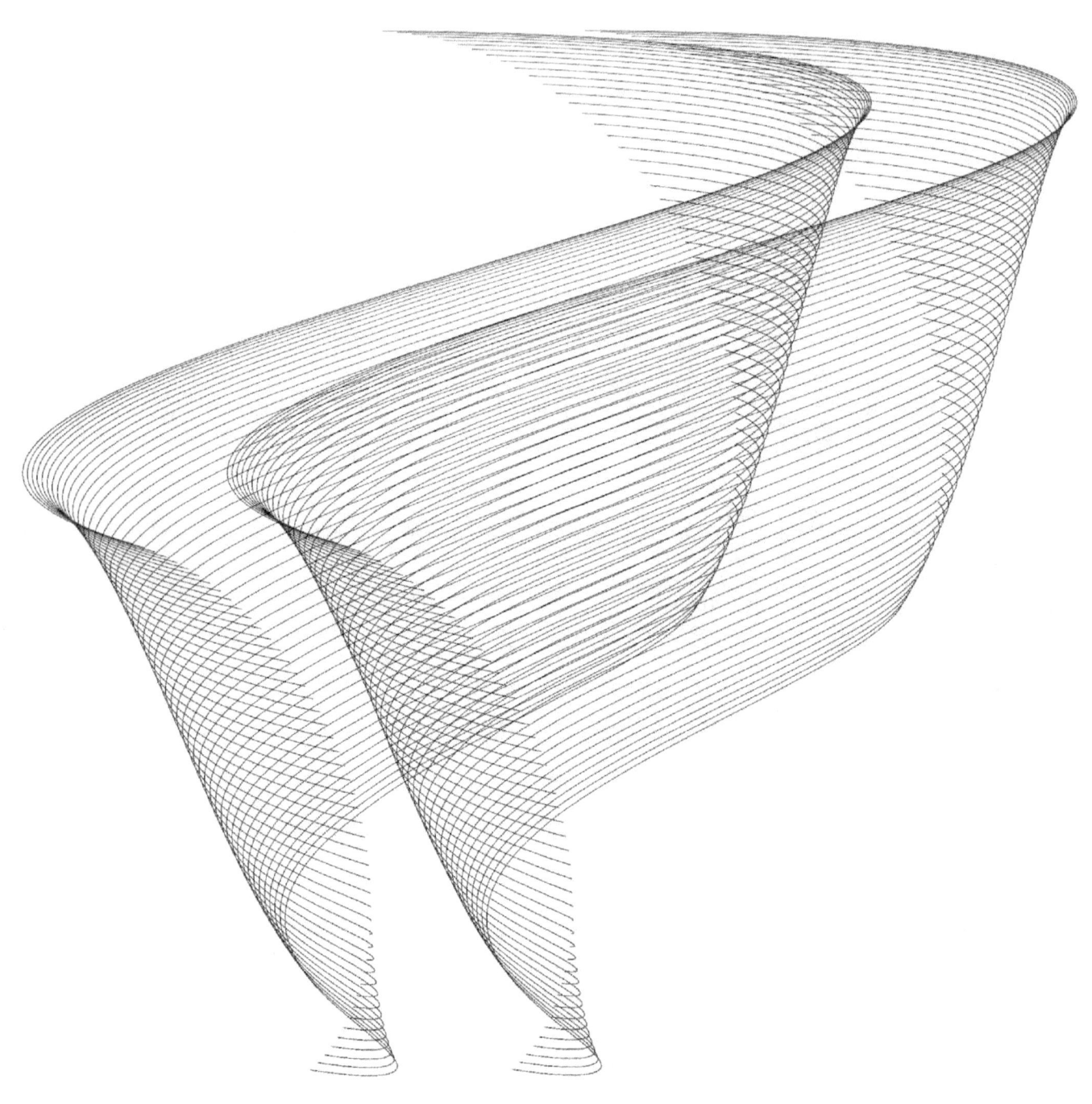

Peace is not absence of conflict.
it is the ability to handle conflict by peaceful means.
Ronald Reagan

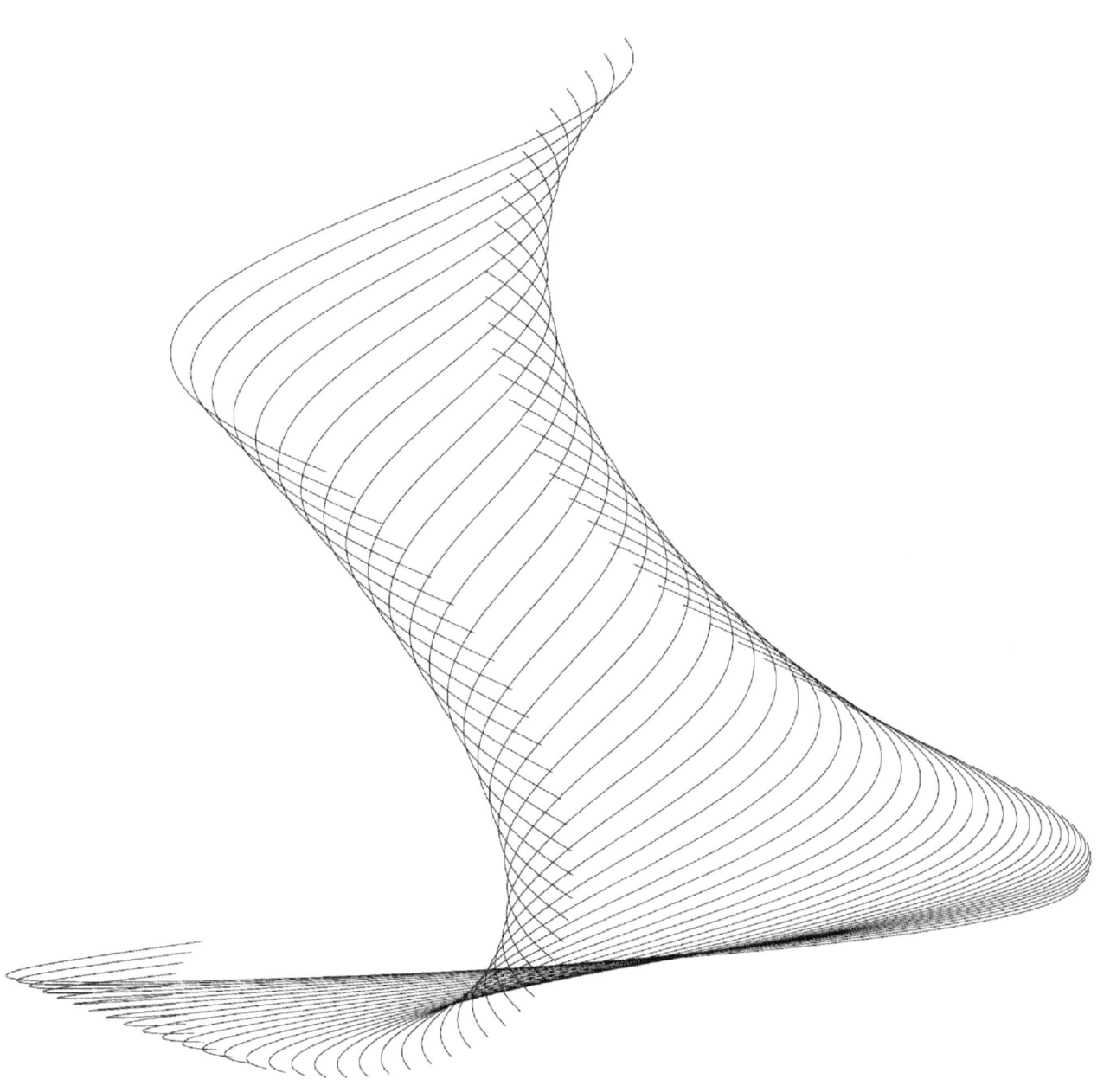

The greatest self is
a peaceful smile, that always sees the world smiling back.
Bryant H. McGi

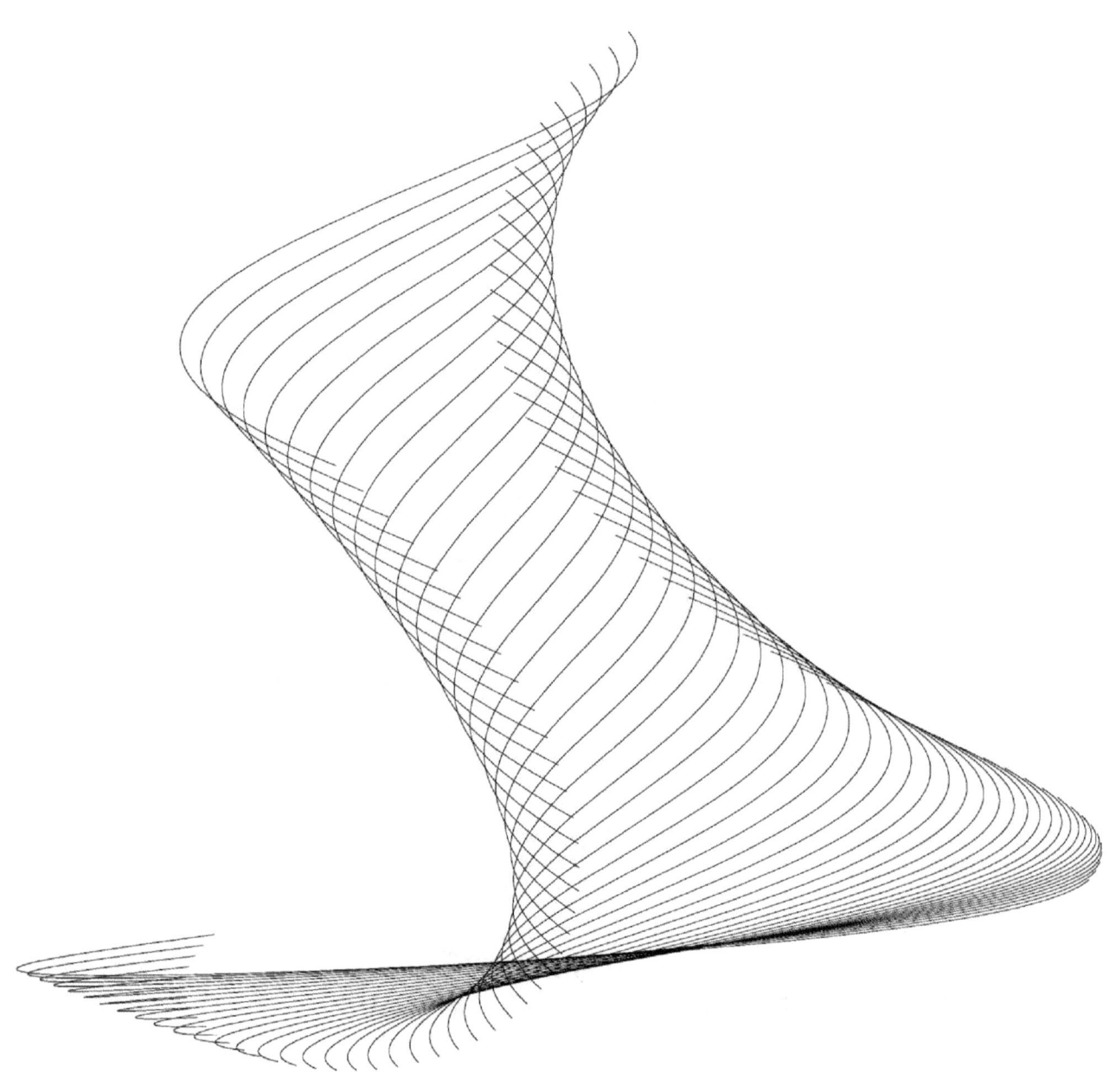

The greatest self is
a peaceful smile, that always sees the world smiling back.
Bryant H. McGi

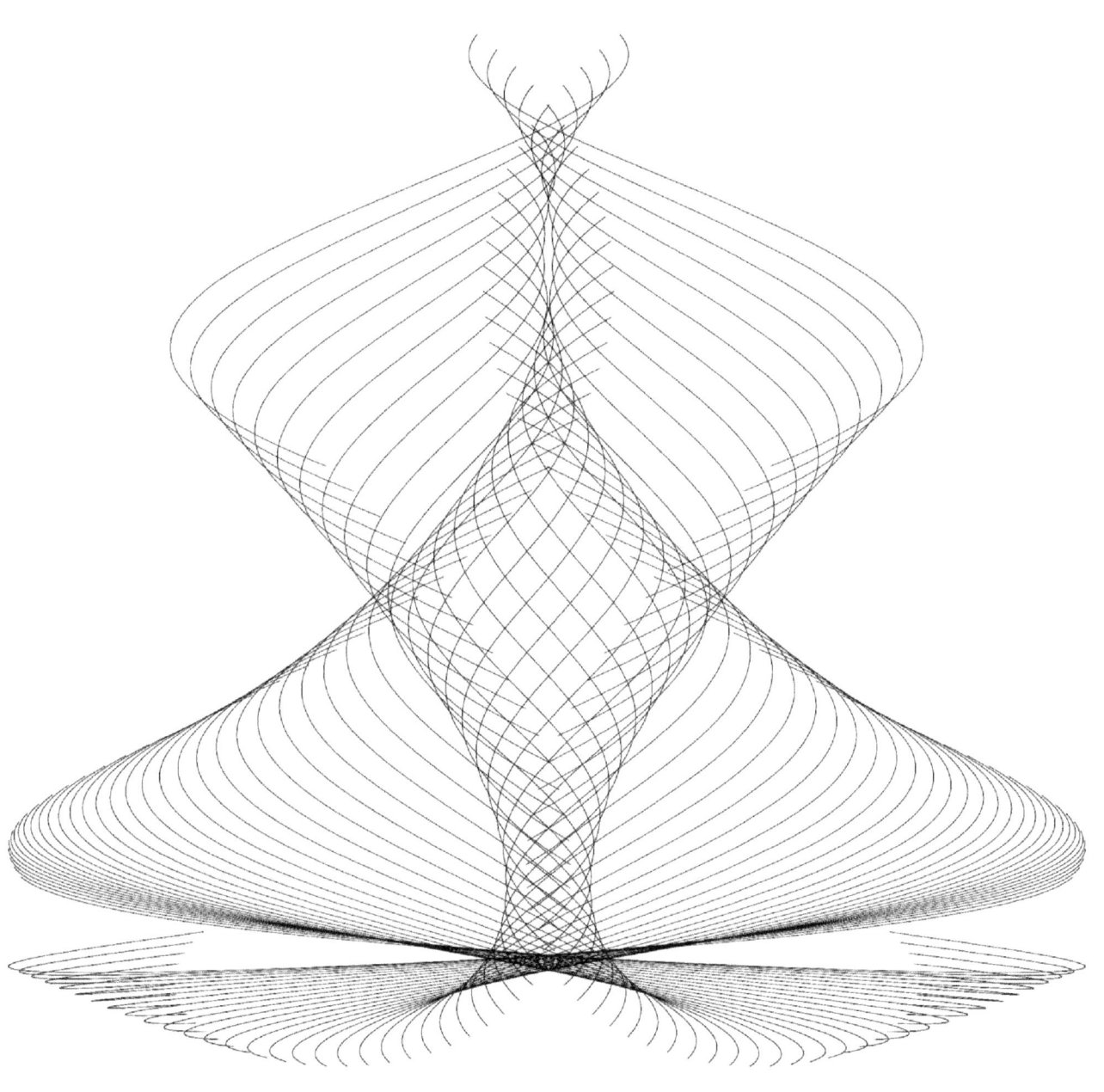

Every gift from a friend is a wish for your happiness.
Richard Bach

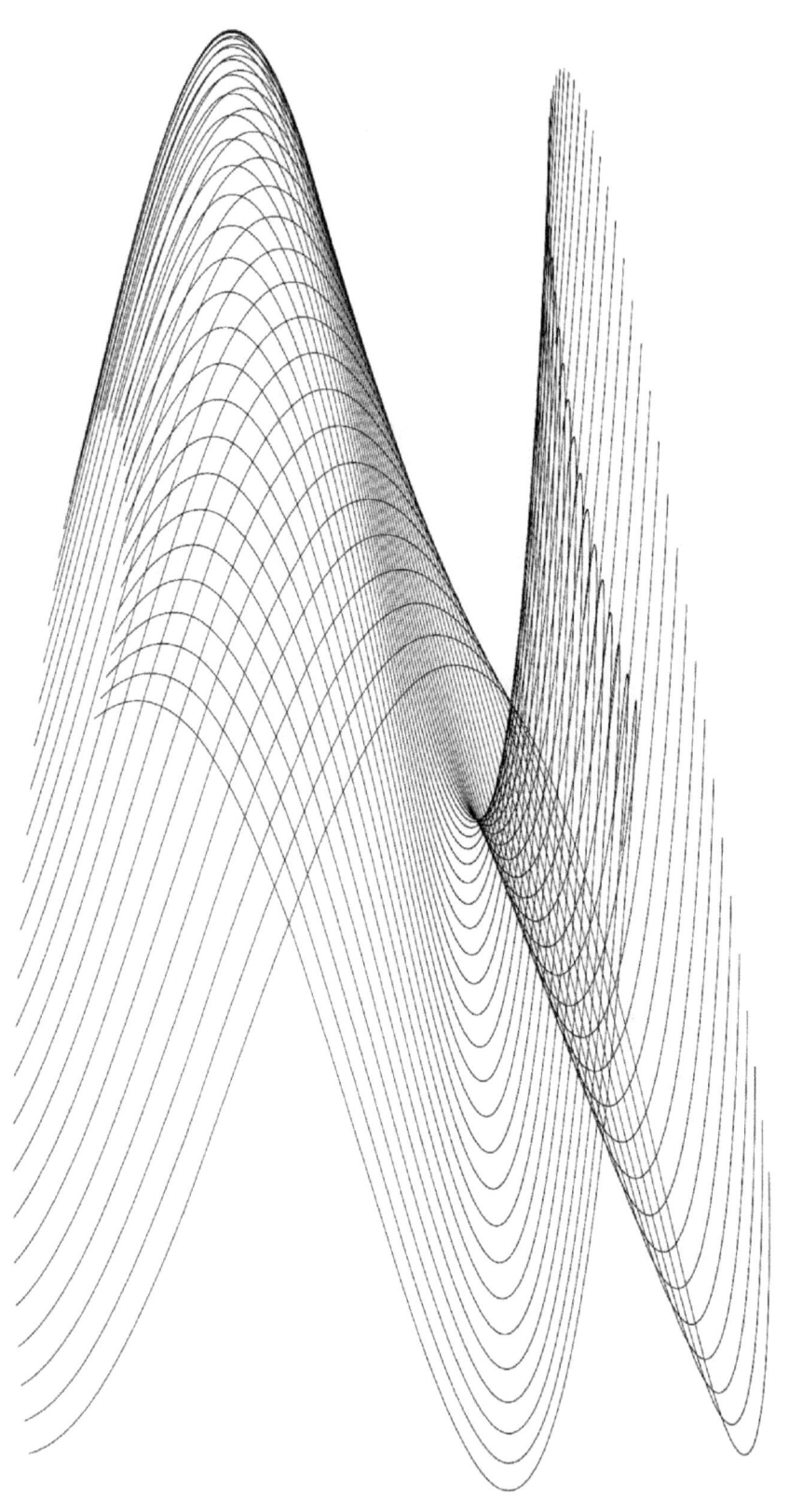

Out of clutter, find simplicity.
Albert Einstein

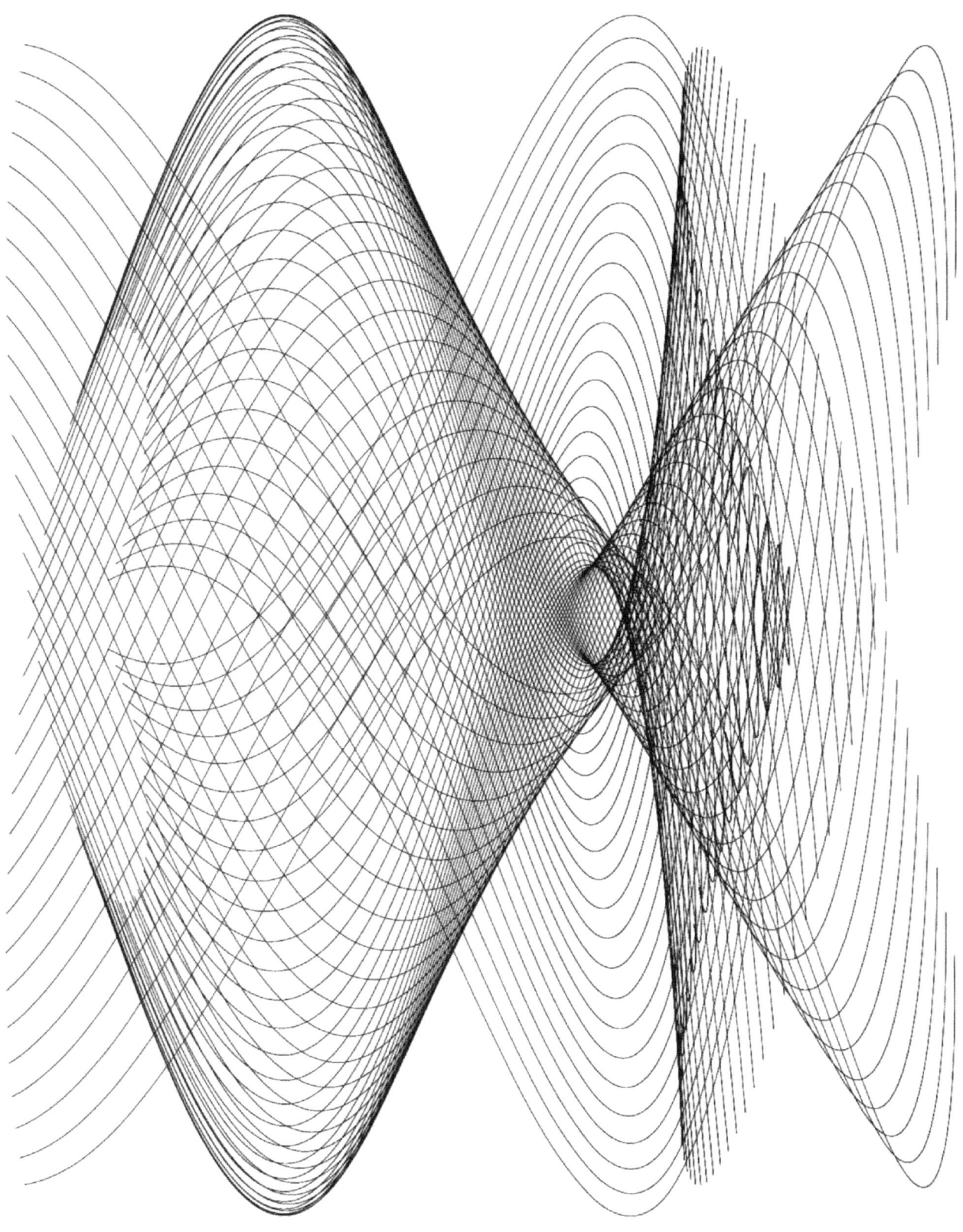

Eat healthily, sleep well, breathe deeply, move harmoniously.
Jean-Pierre Barral

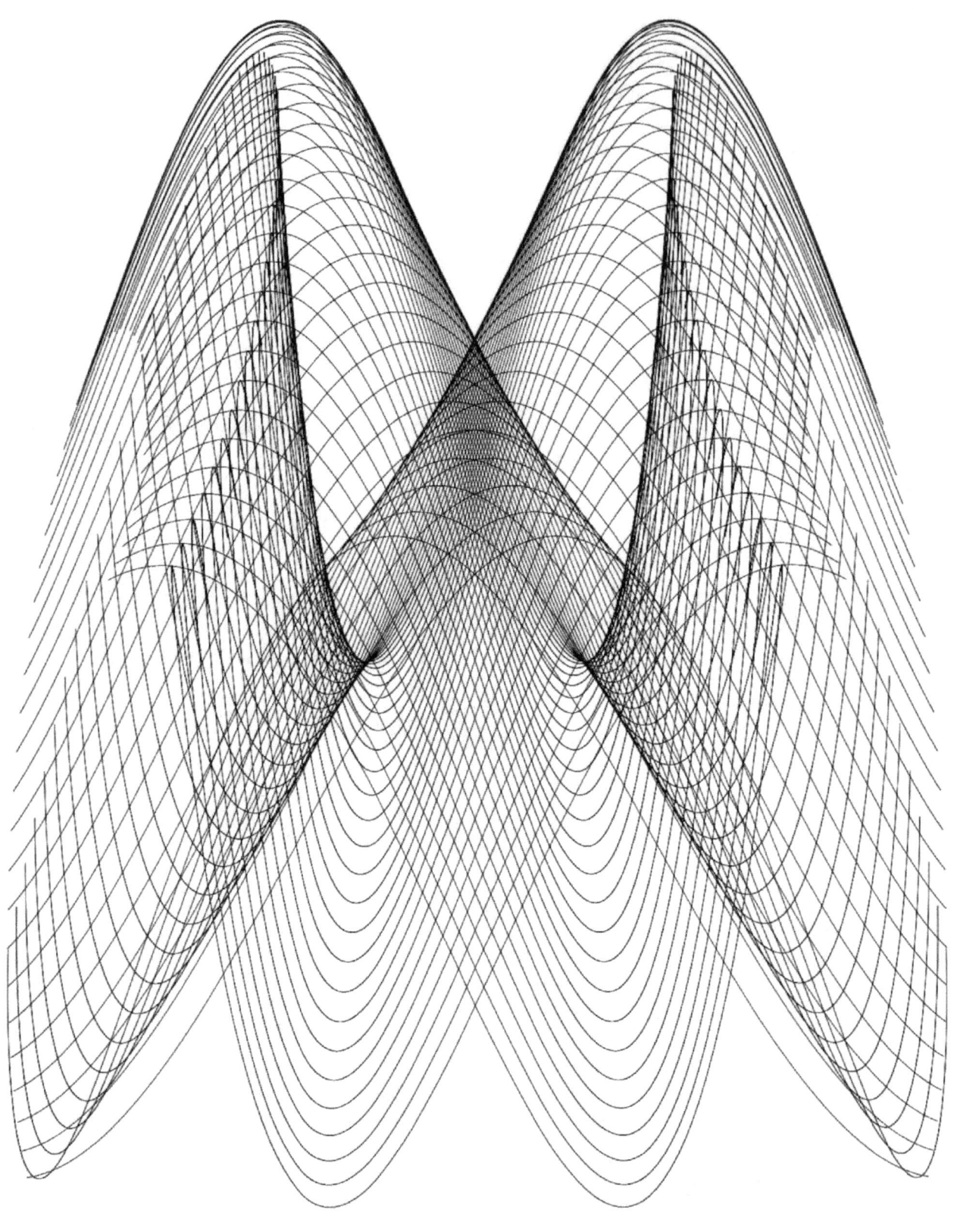

You are only afraid if you are not in harmony with yourself.
Hermann Hesse

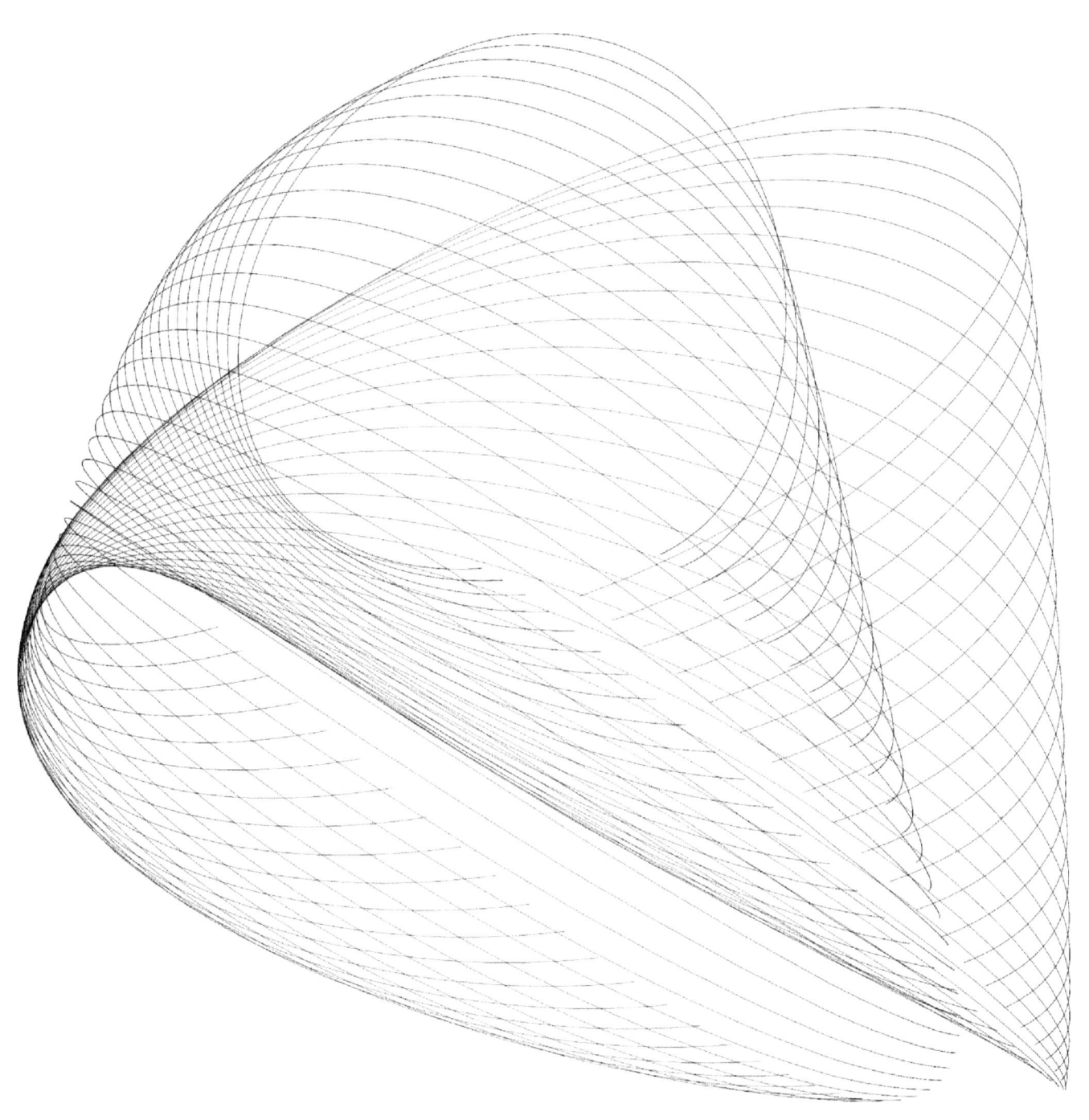

All matters being spiritual:
man or woman can only find peace when
peace is realized from within.
T. F. Hodge

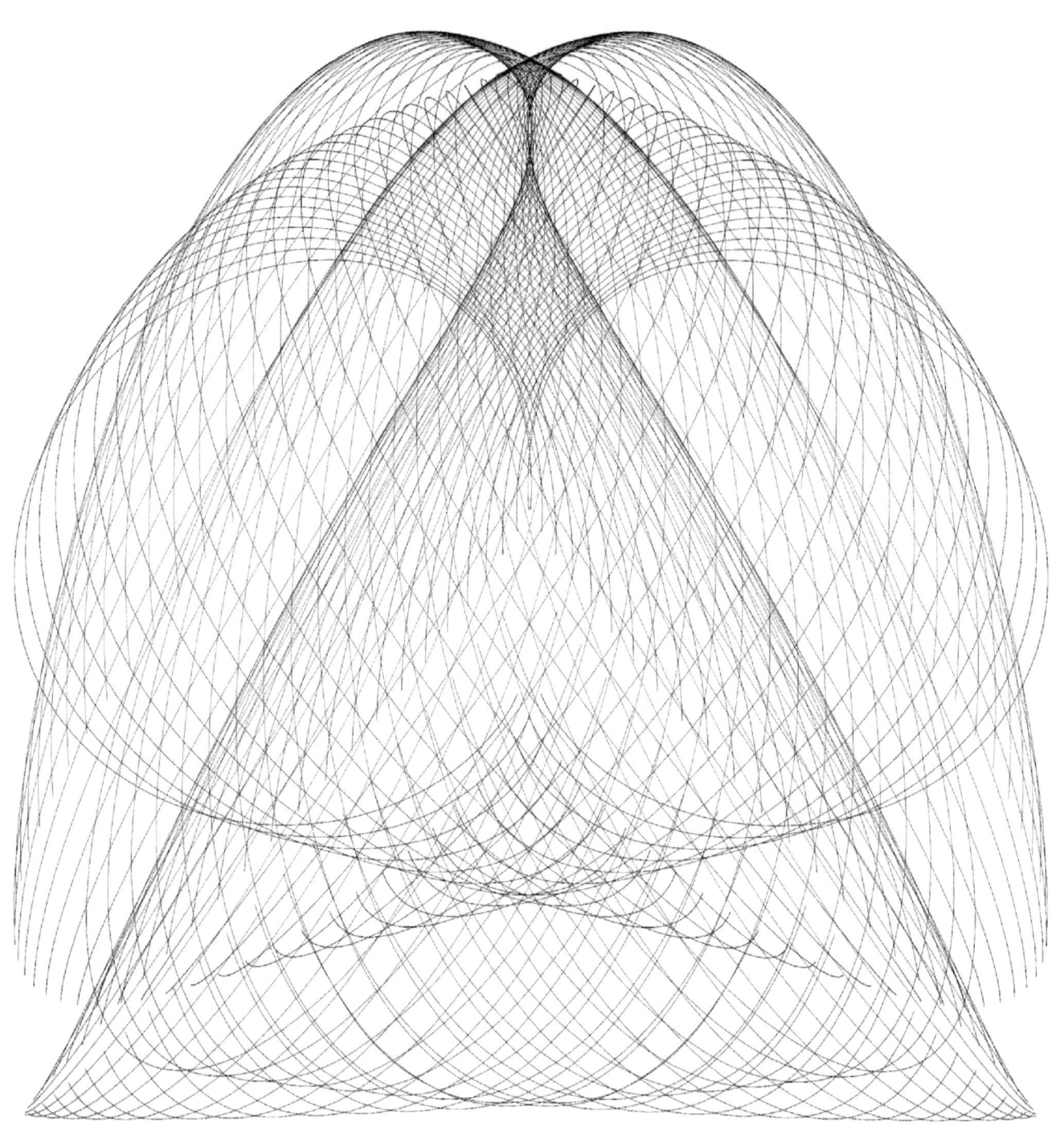

Digressions are part of harmony, deviations too.
Dejan Stojanovic

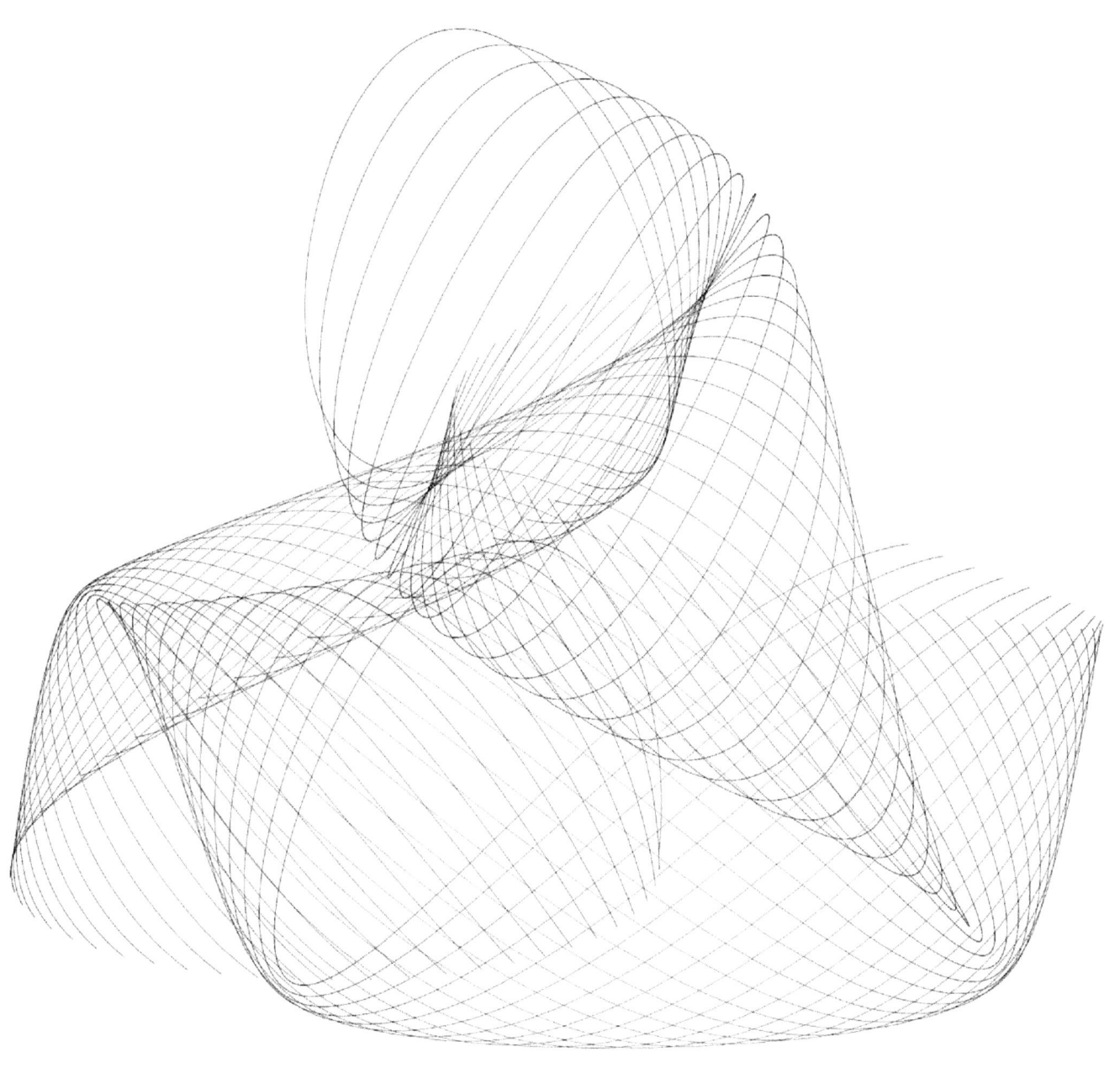

To understand and be understood is to be at peace.
Kamand Kojouri

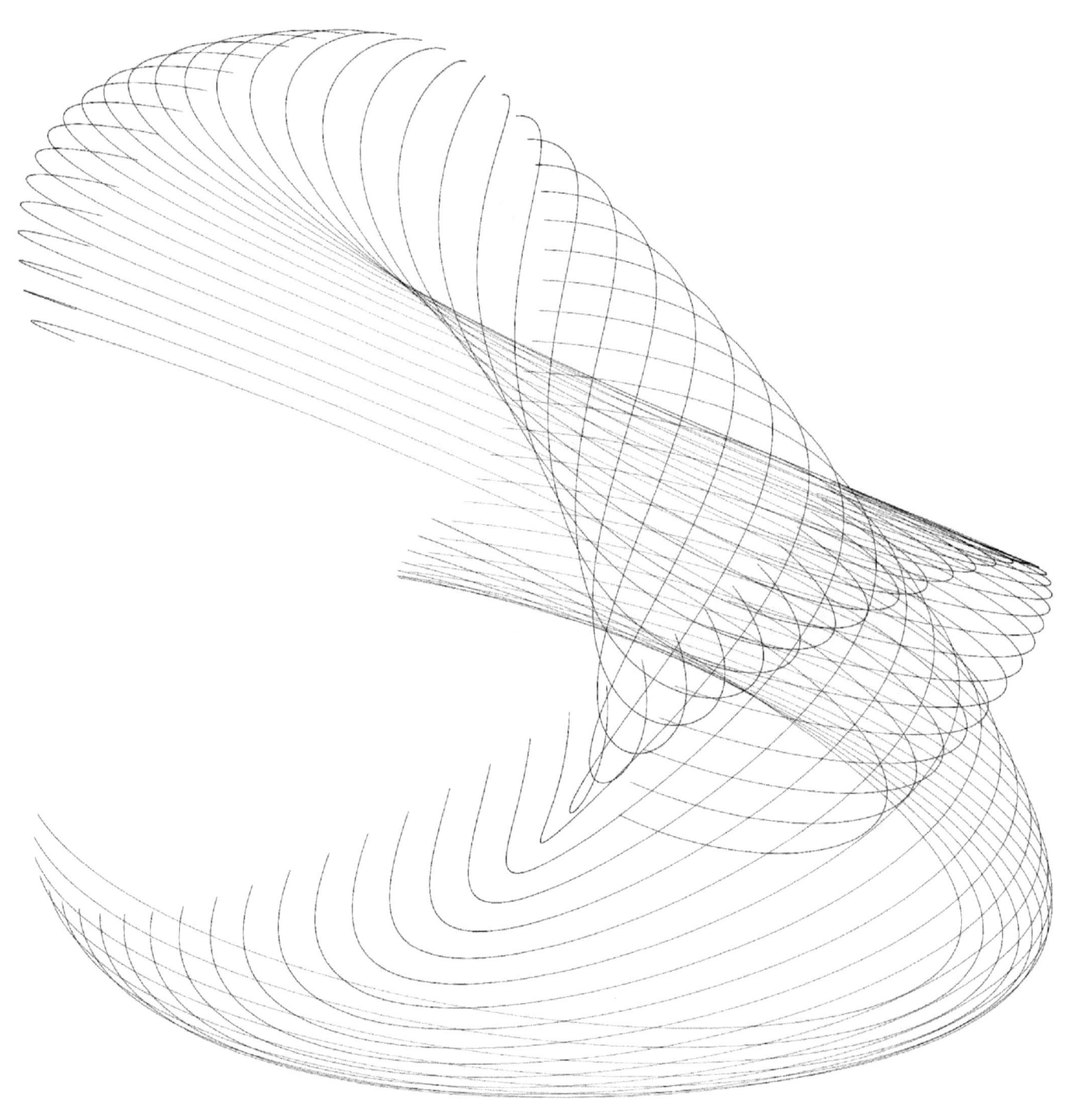

Wonderment shared is doubled.
Love shared is infinite.
Kamand Kojouri

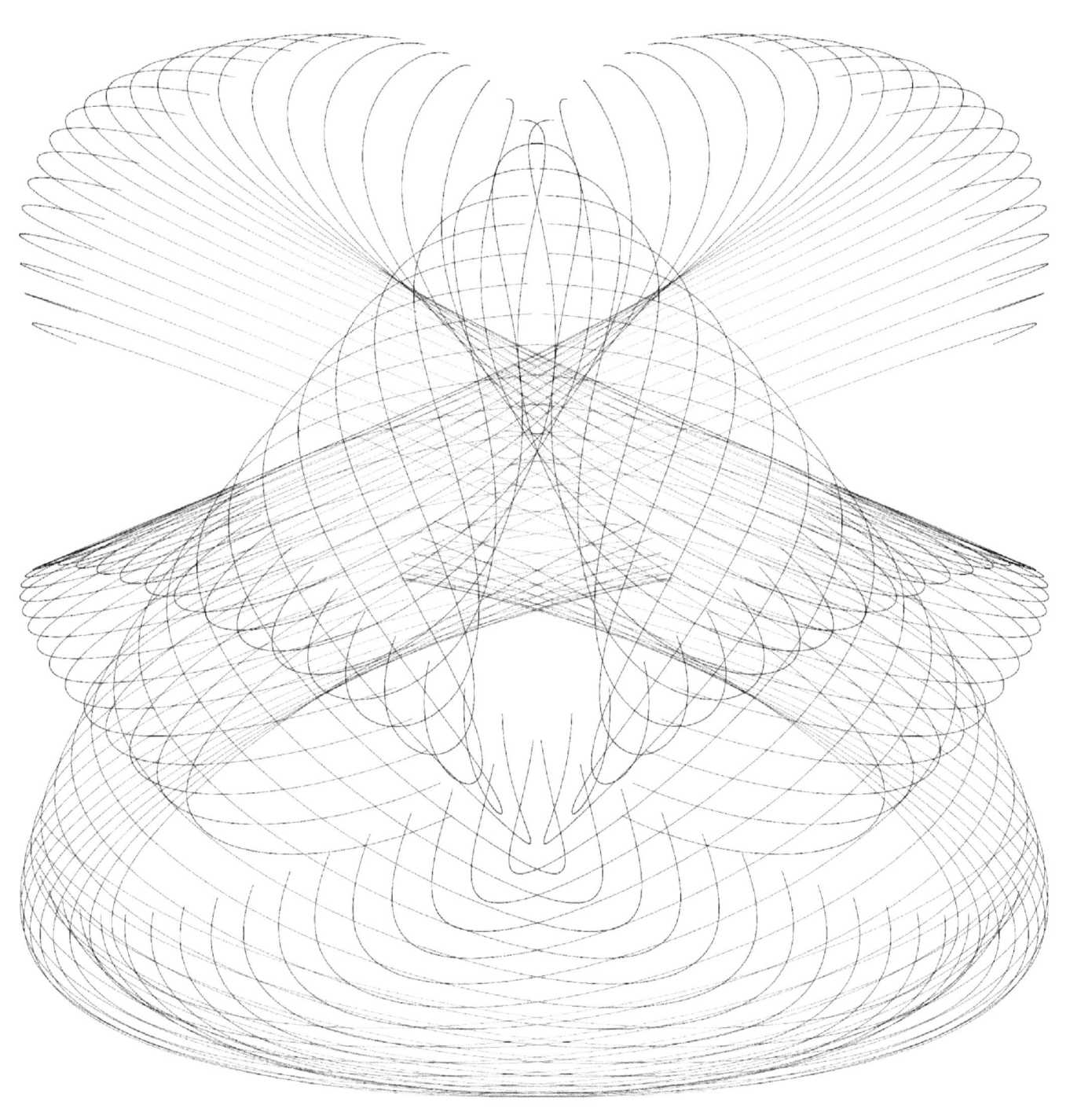

Like nature, we must grow with
tranquility, beauty, harmony, and love. "
Debasish Mridha

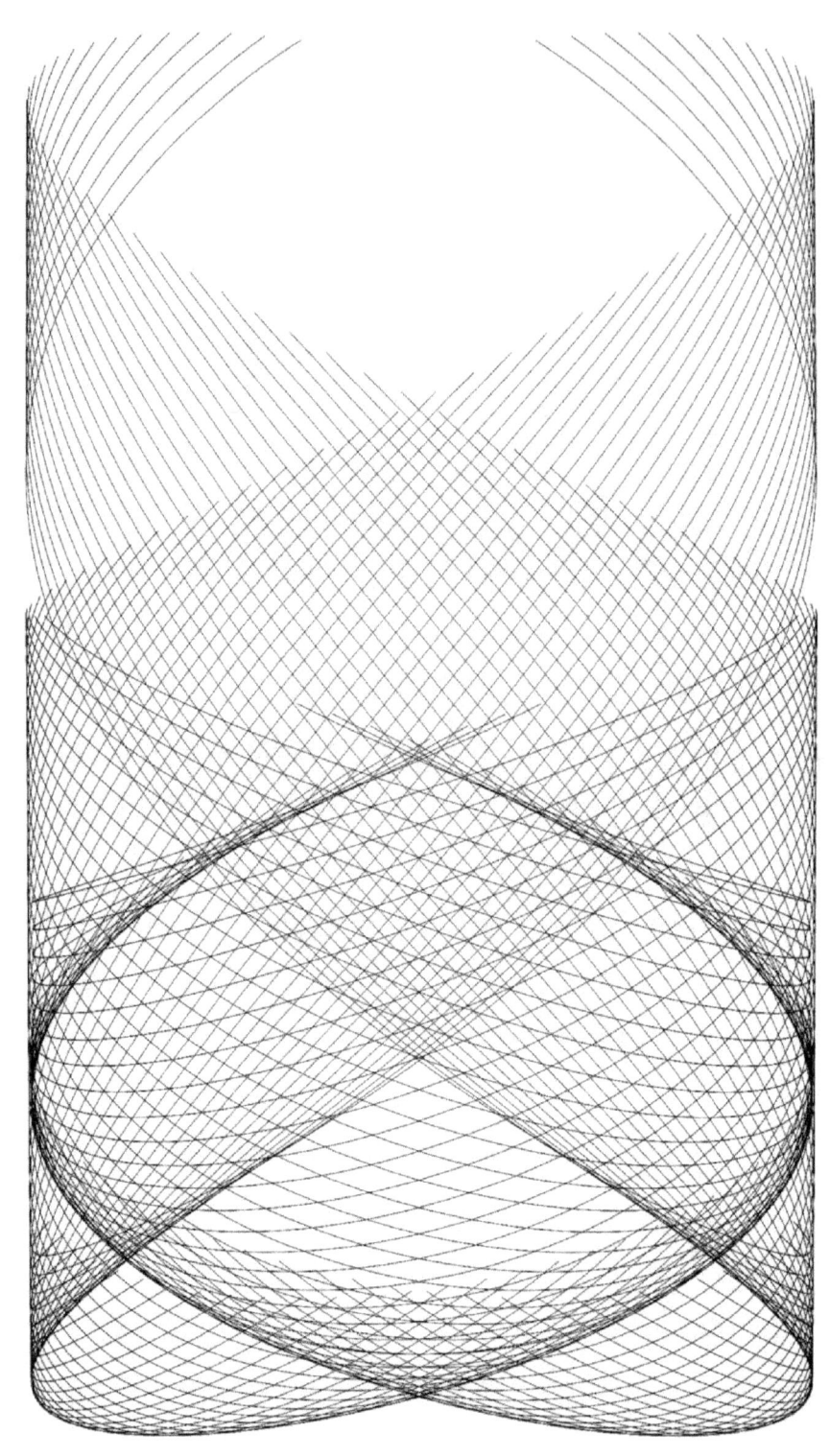

Wherever your heart is,
that is where you´ll find your treasure
Paulo Cohelo

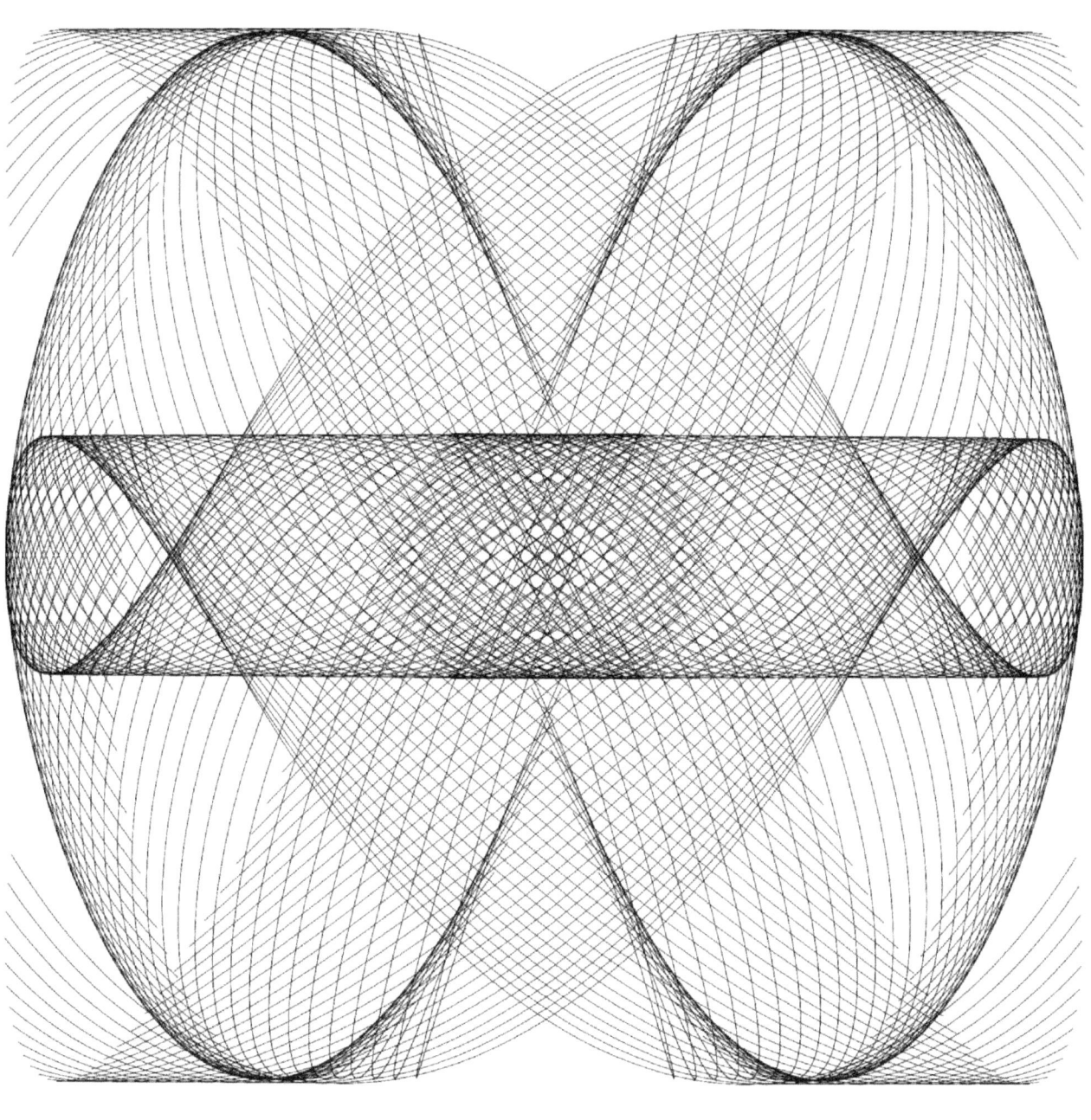

Love is the opposite of fear
and it lights the flames of a million hearts
Amy Leigh Mercree

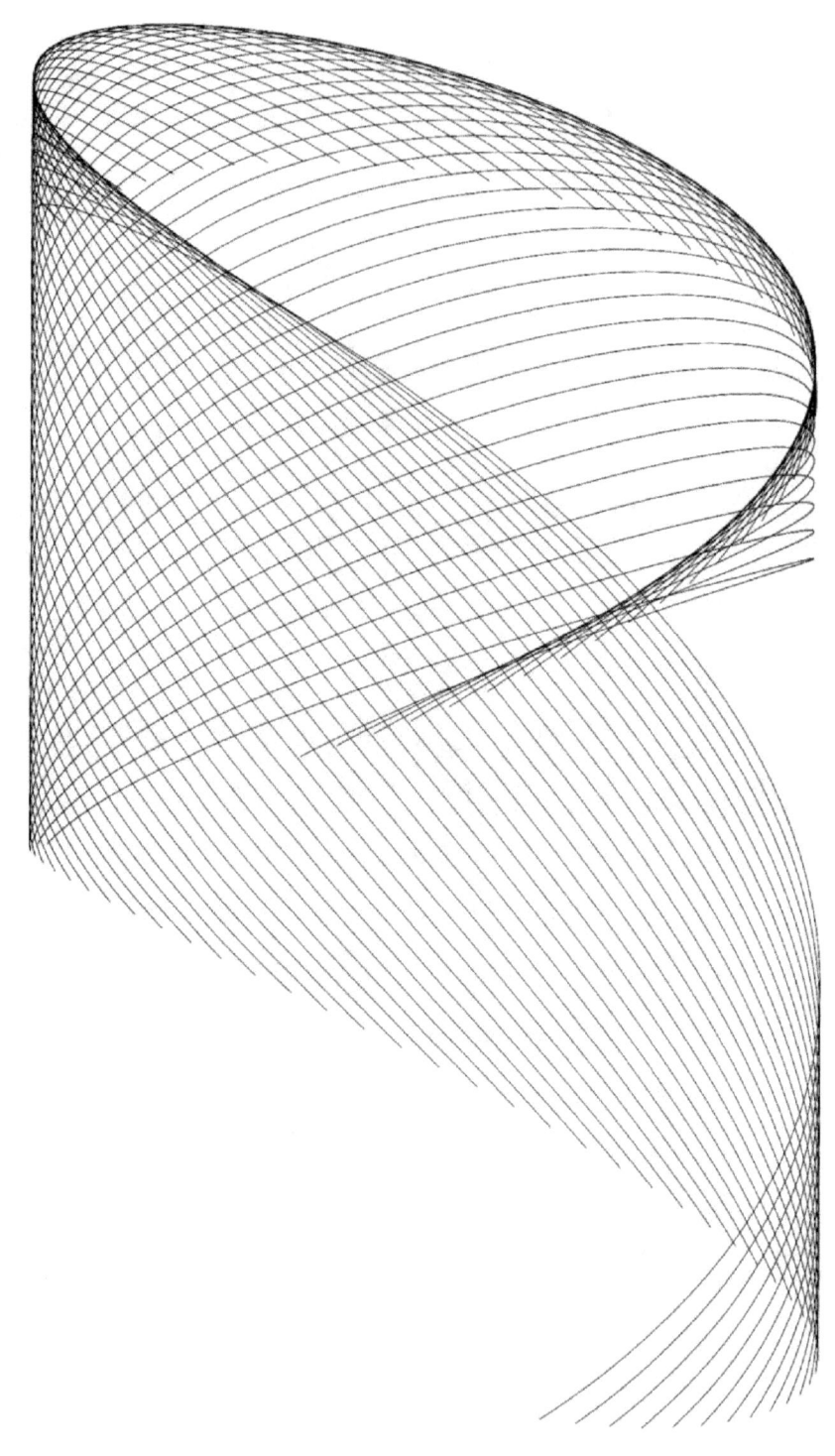

Do your work, then step back. The only path to serenity
Lao Tzu

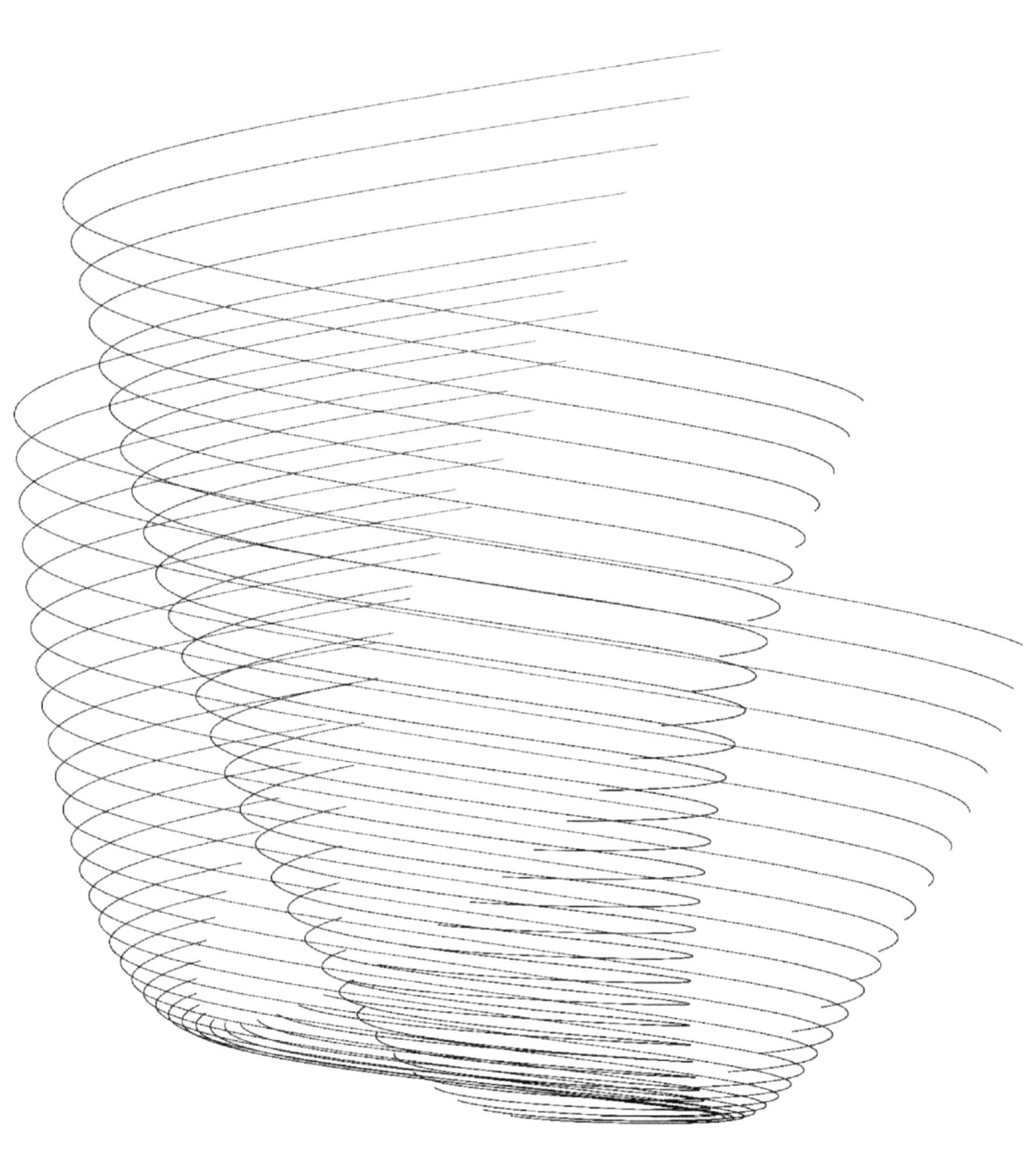

Go in the direction of where your peace is coming from.
C. JoyBell C.

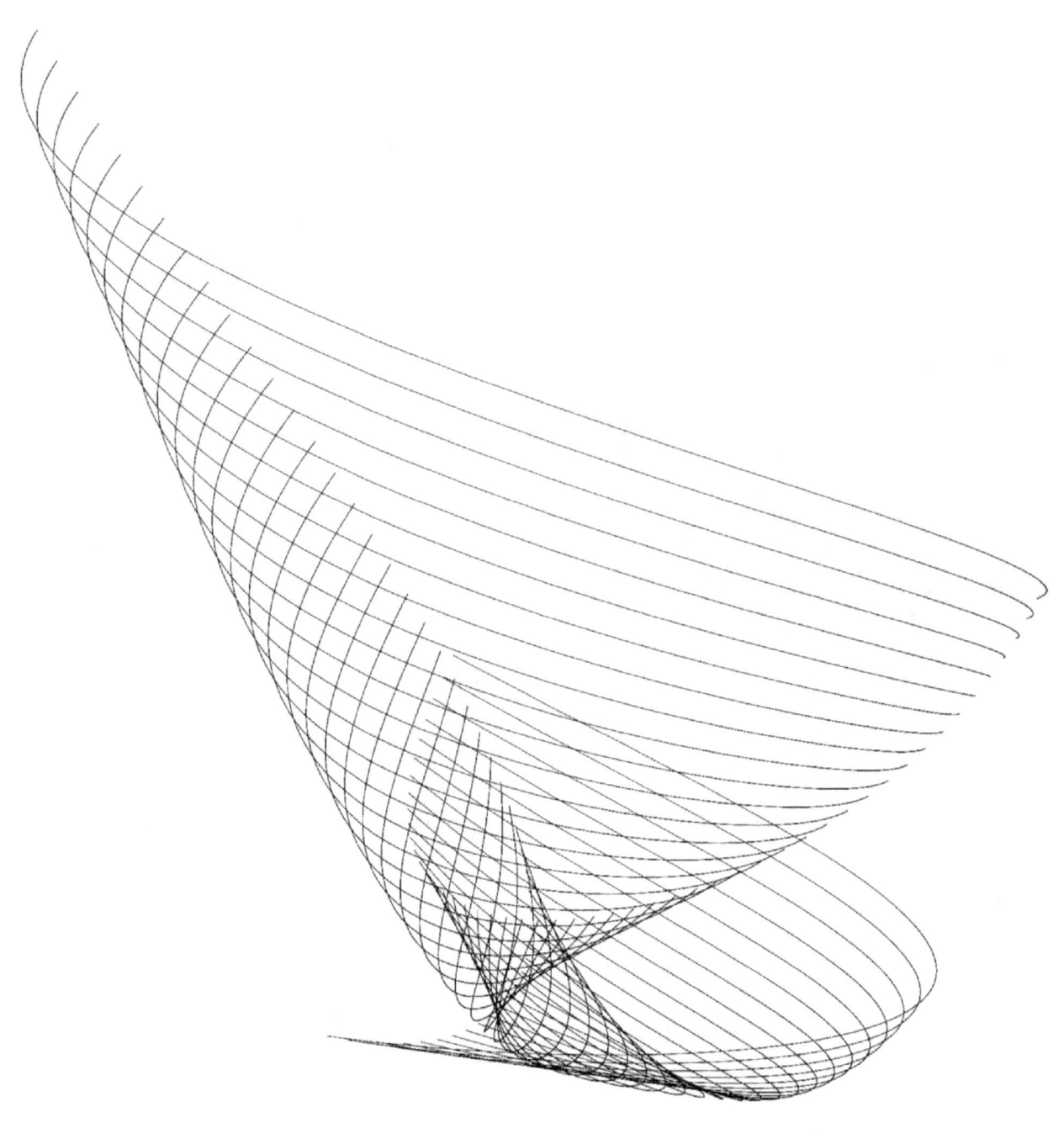

Change what cannot be accepted and accept what cannot be changed.
Reinhold Niebuhr

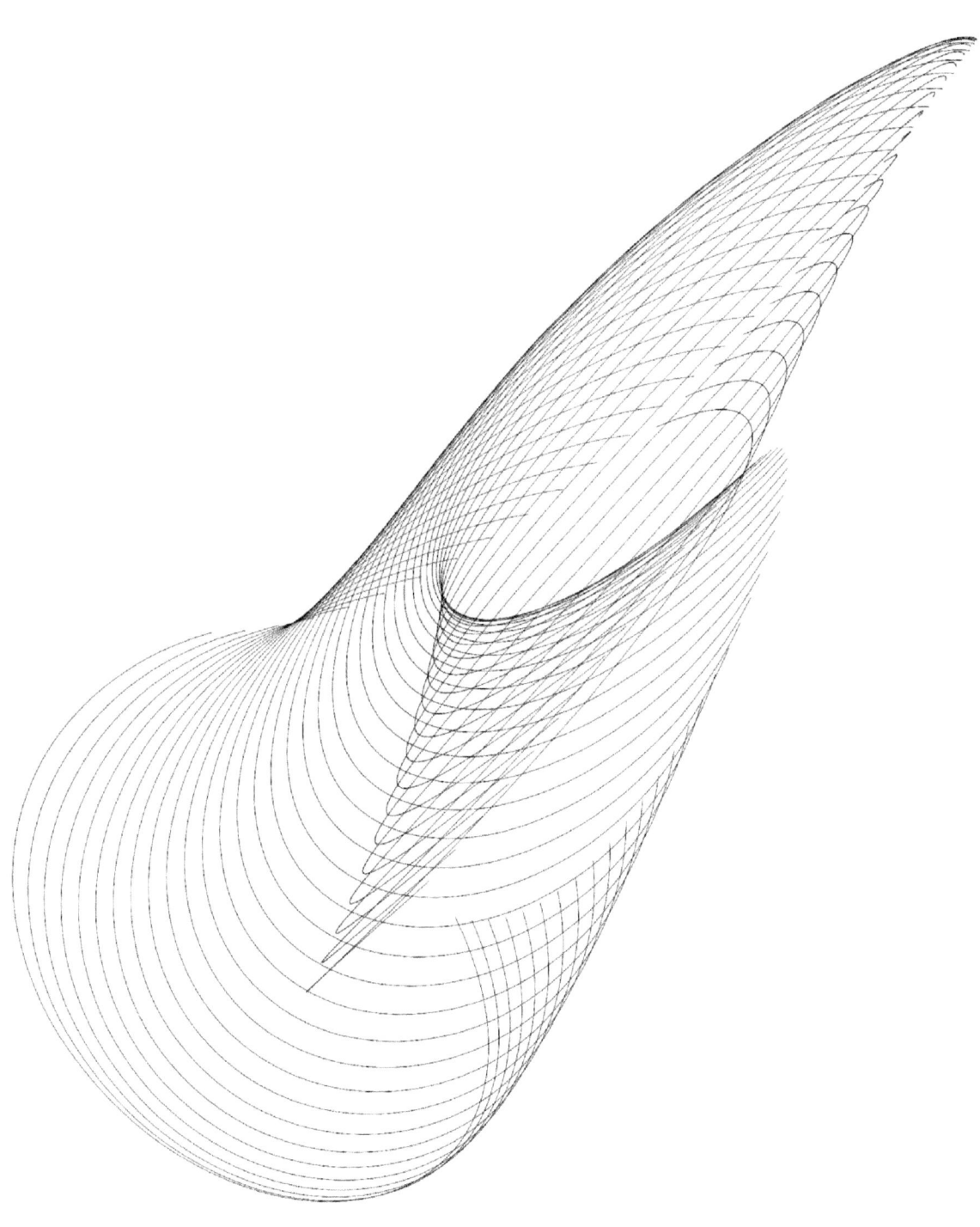

Do not allow outer chaos disturb
your inner tranquility, serenity, and peace.
Debasish Mridha

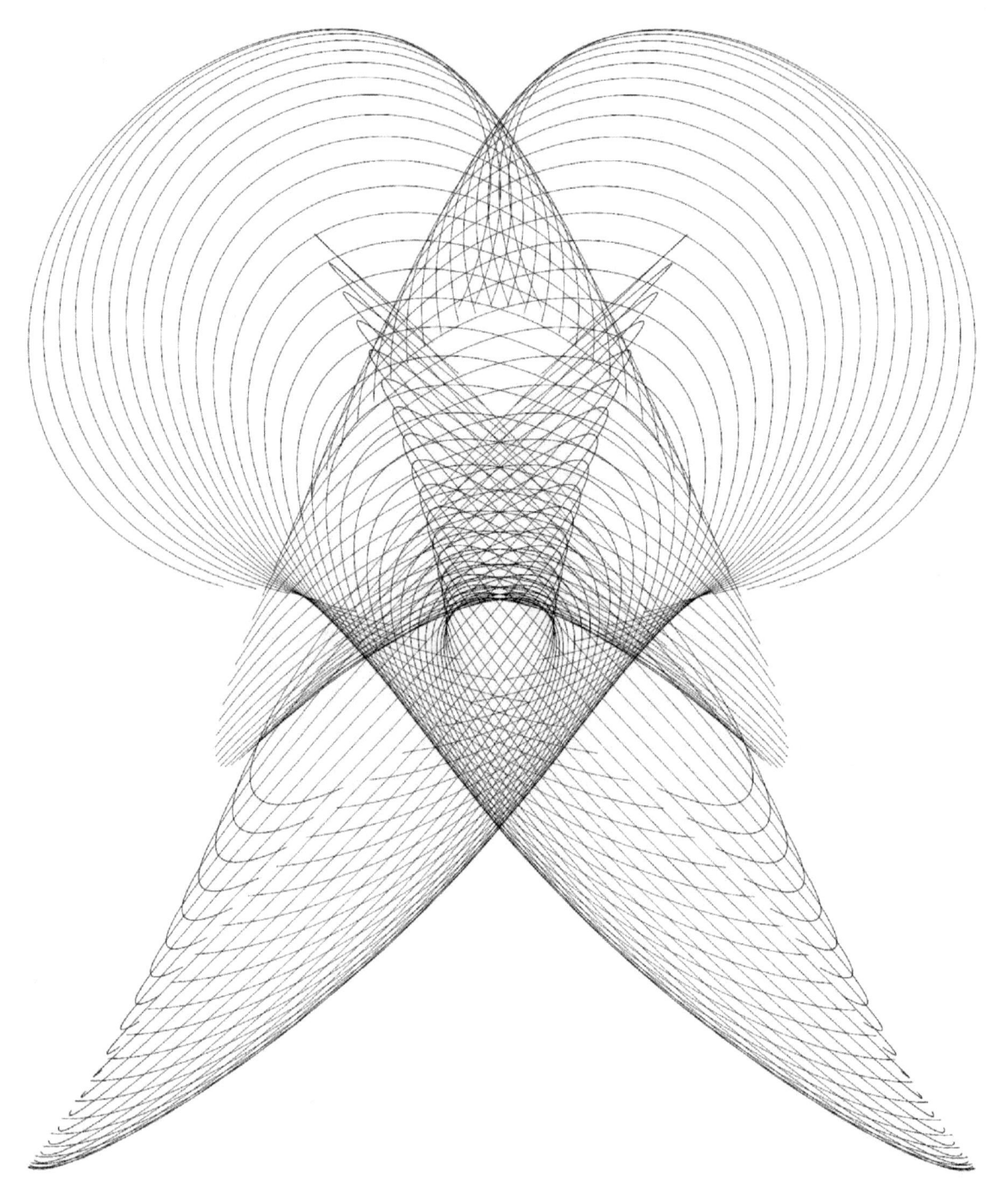

You were beautifully and wonderfully created
with the skin of diamonds, so if you do break, you are still valuable.
Courtney Brooks

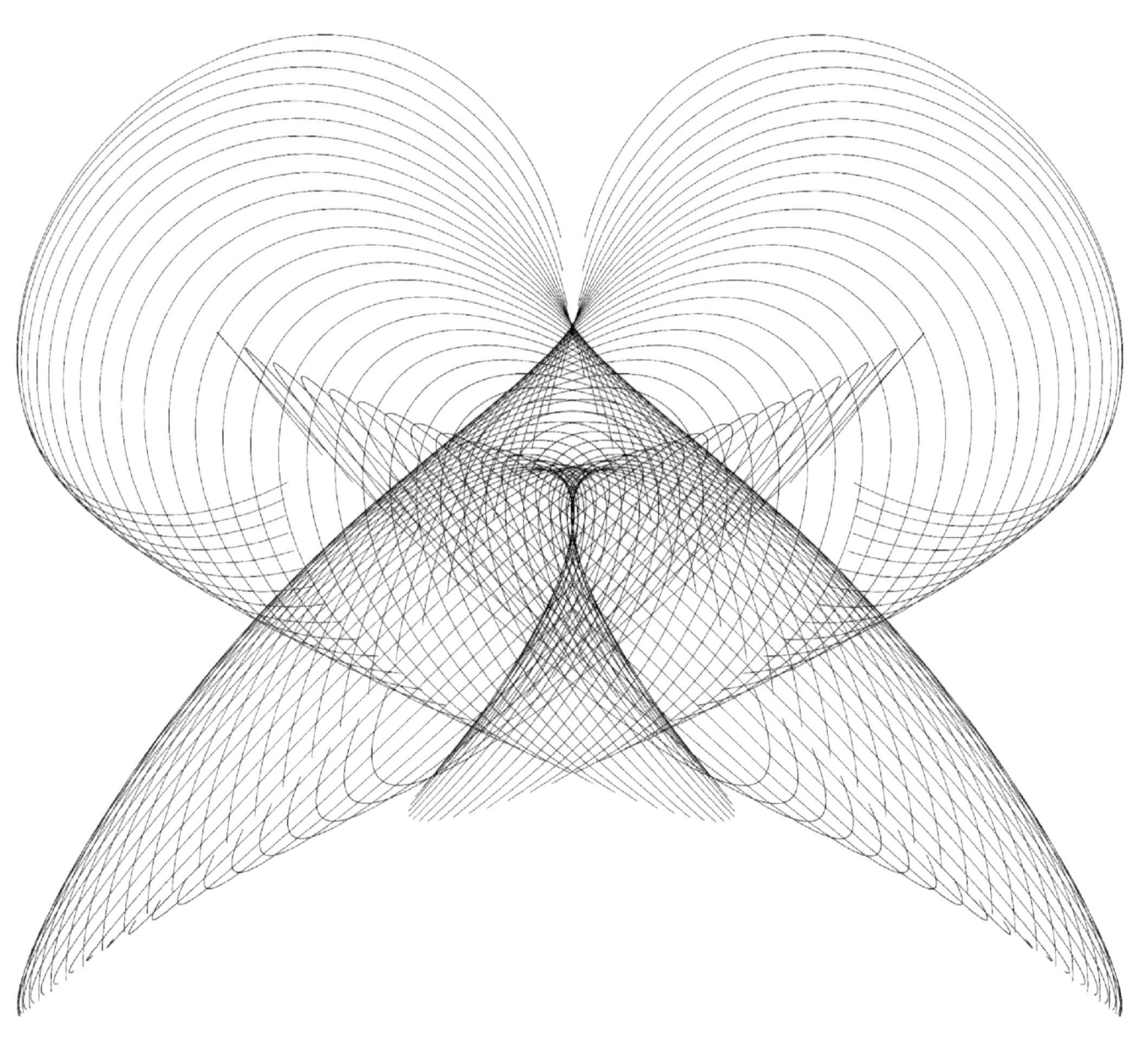

Live each day with ecstatic serenity
Lailah Gifty Akita

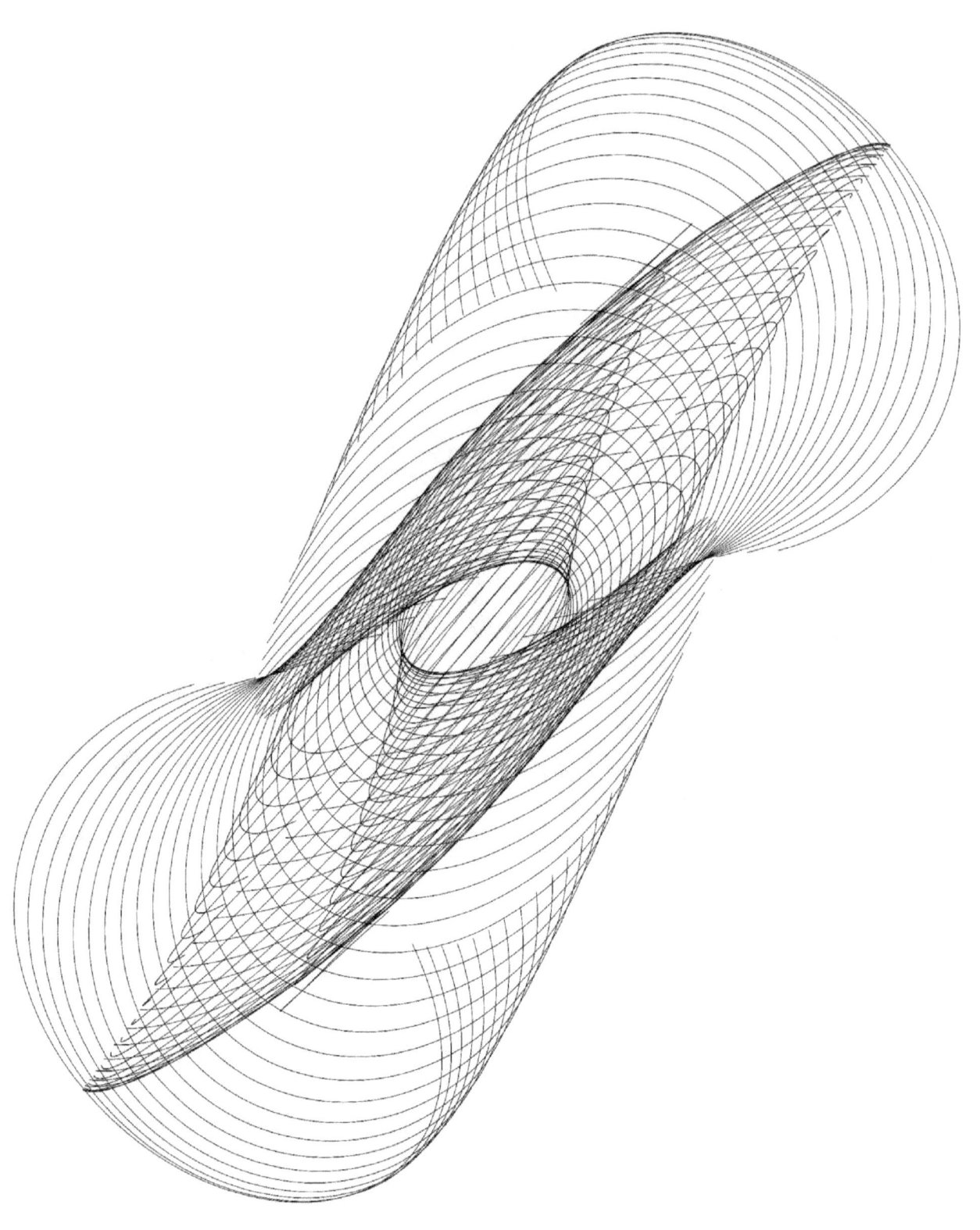

I like the night.
Without the dark, we'd never see the stars.
Stephenie Meyer

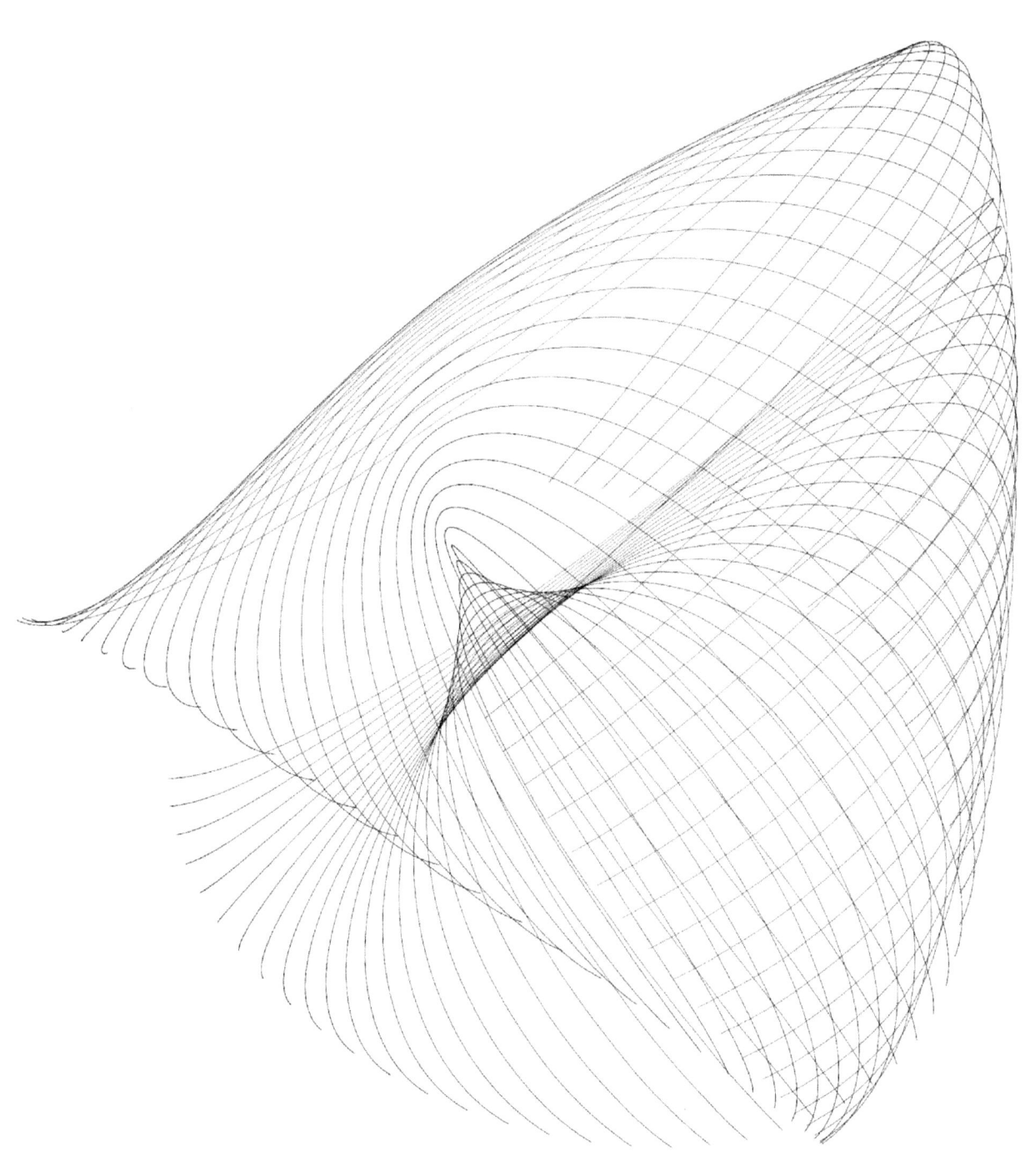

Don't cry because it's over, smile because it happened.
Dr. Seuss

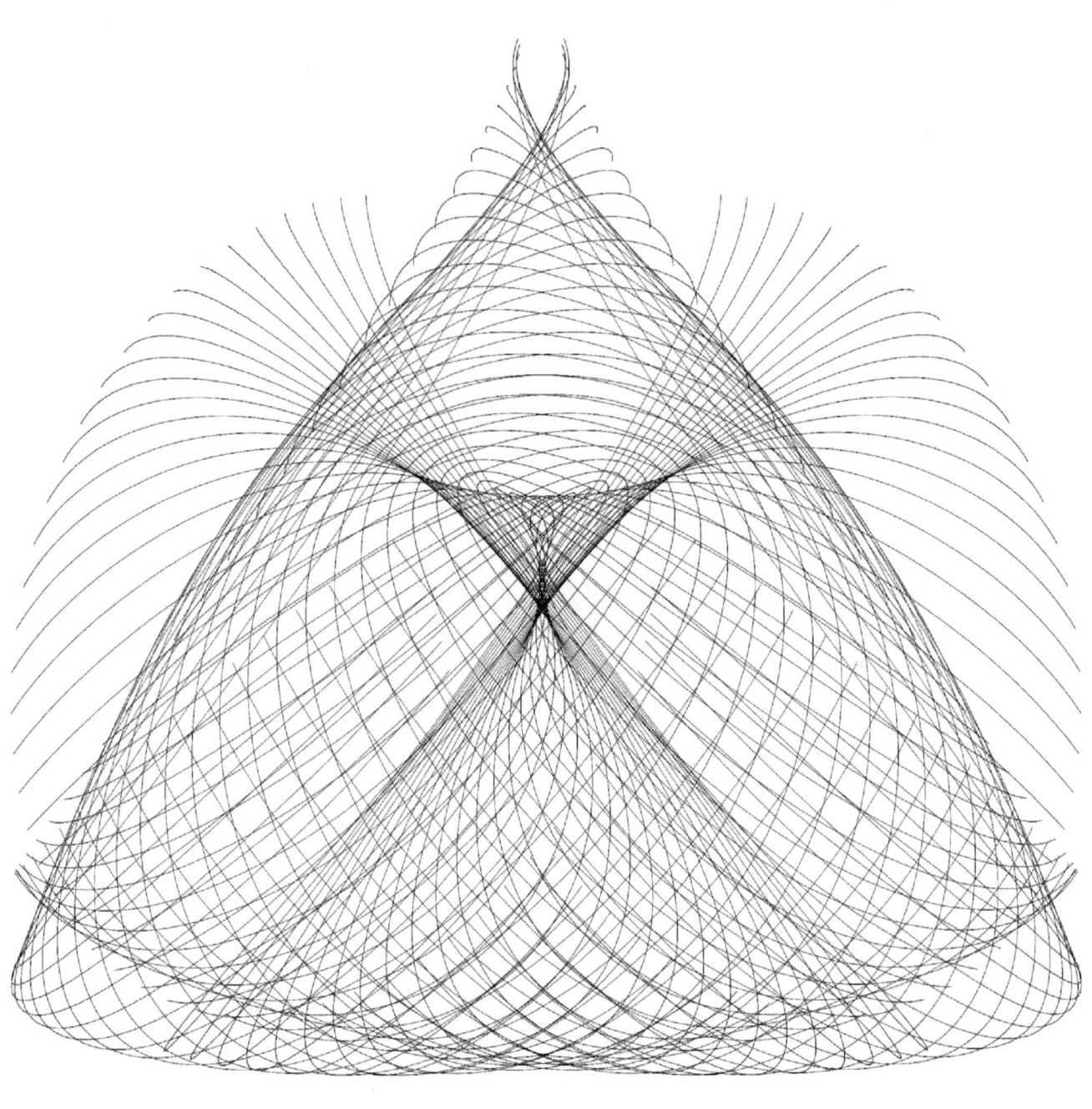

Count your age by friends, not years. Count your life by smiles, not tears.
John Lennon

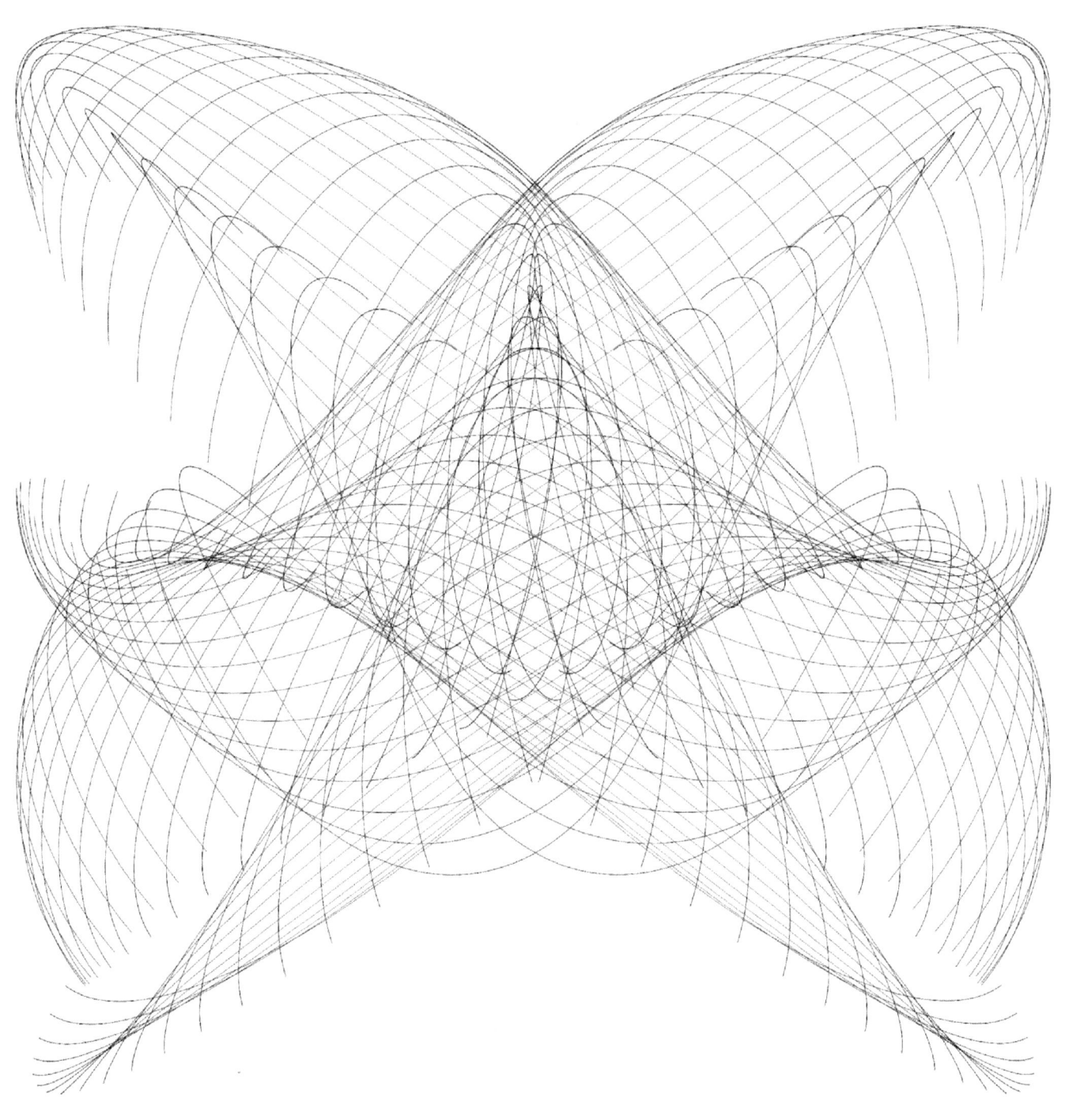

Sanity and happiness are an impossible combination.
Mark Twain

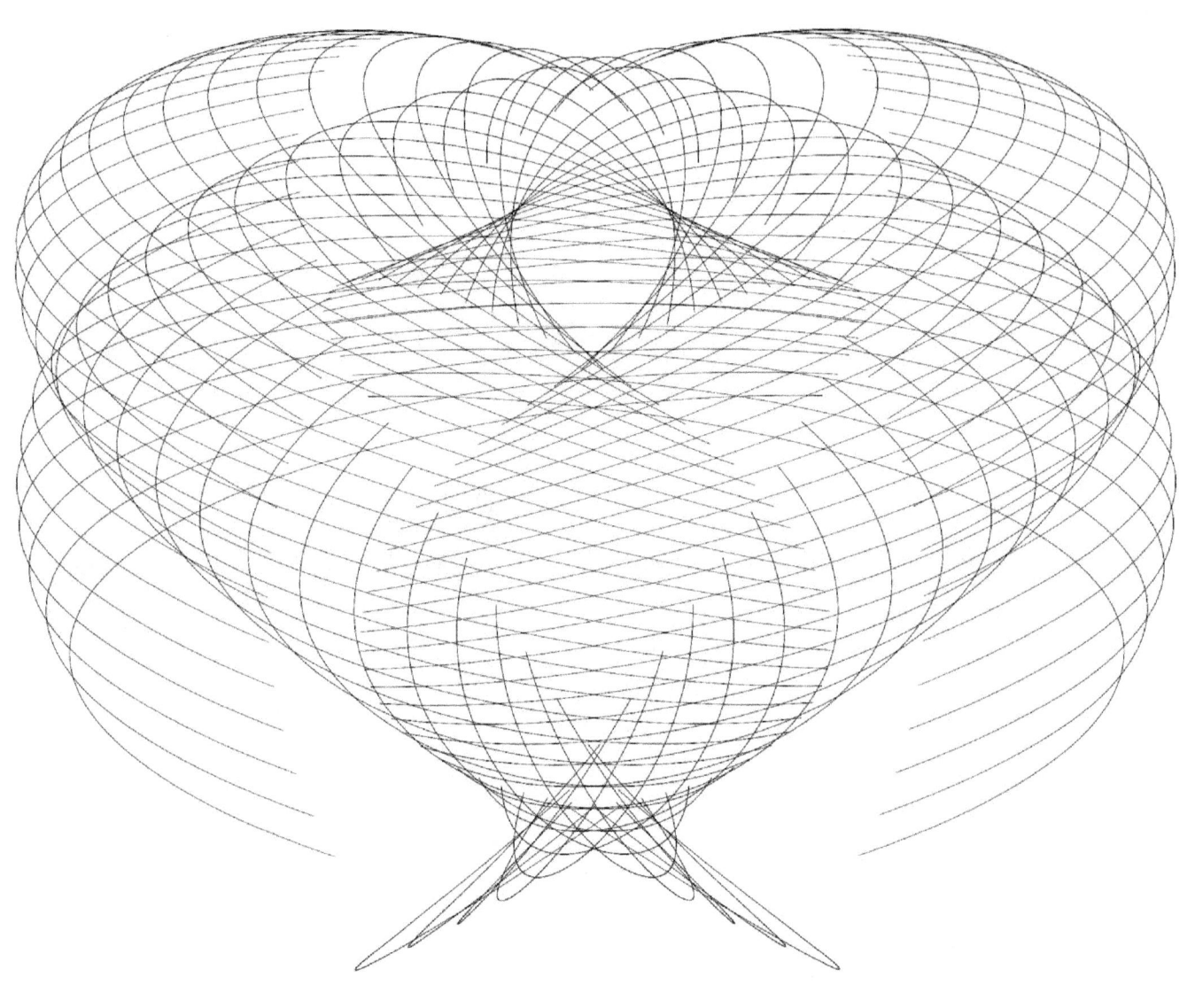

The most wasted of all days is one without laughter.
Nicolas Chamfort

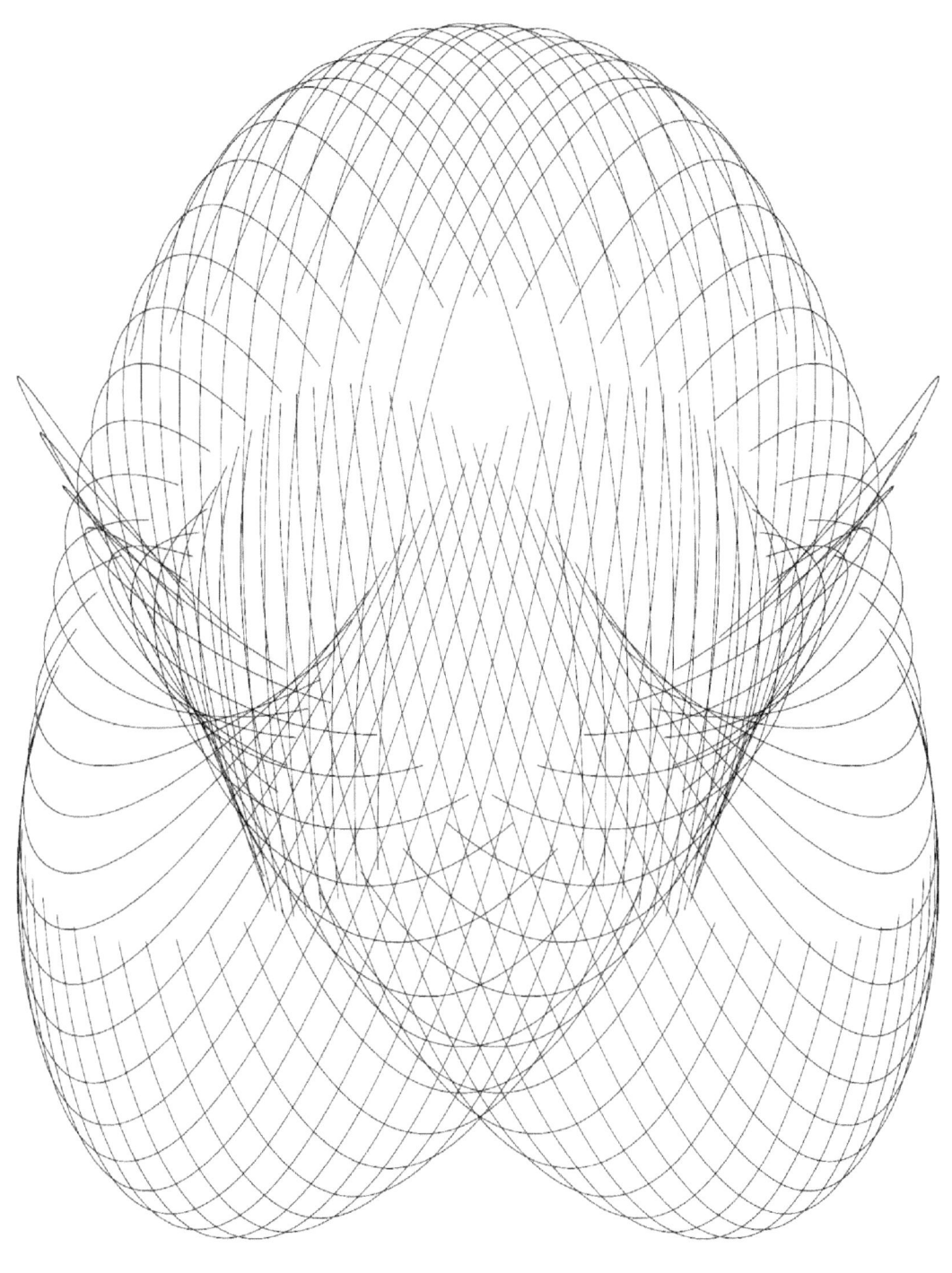

One can never consent to creep when one feels an impulse to soar.
Helen Keller

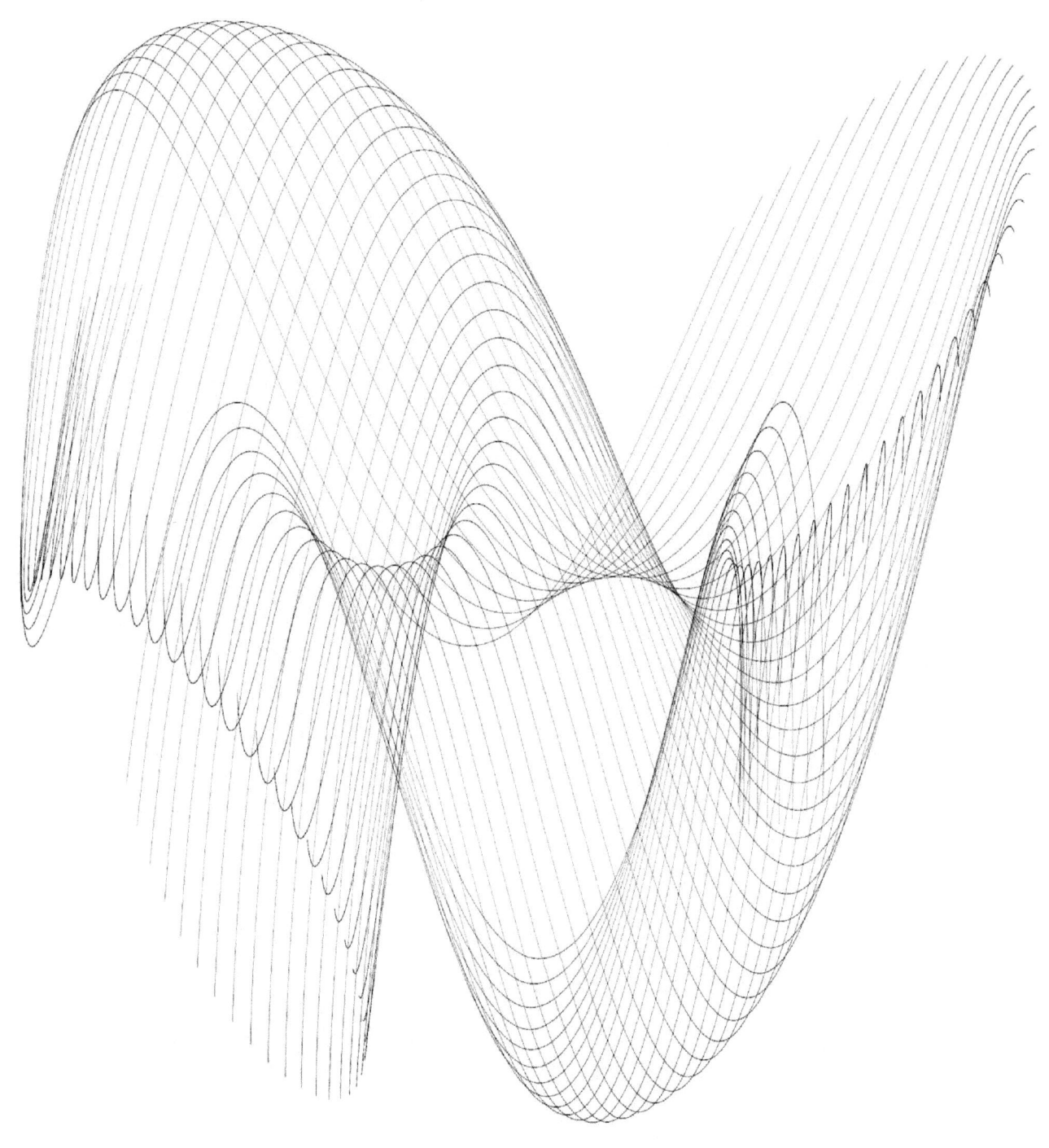

Comparison is the death of joy.
Mark Twain

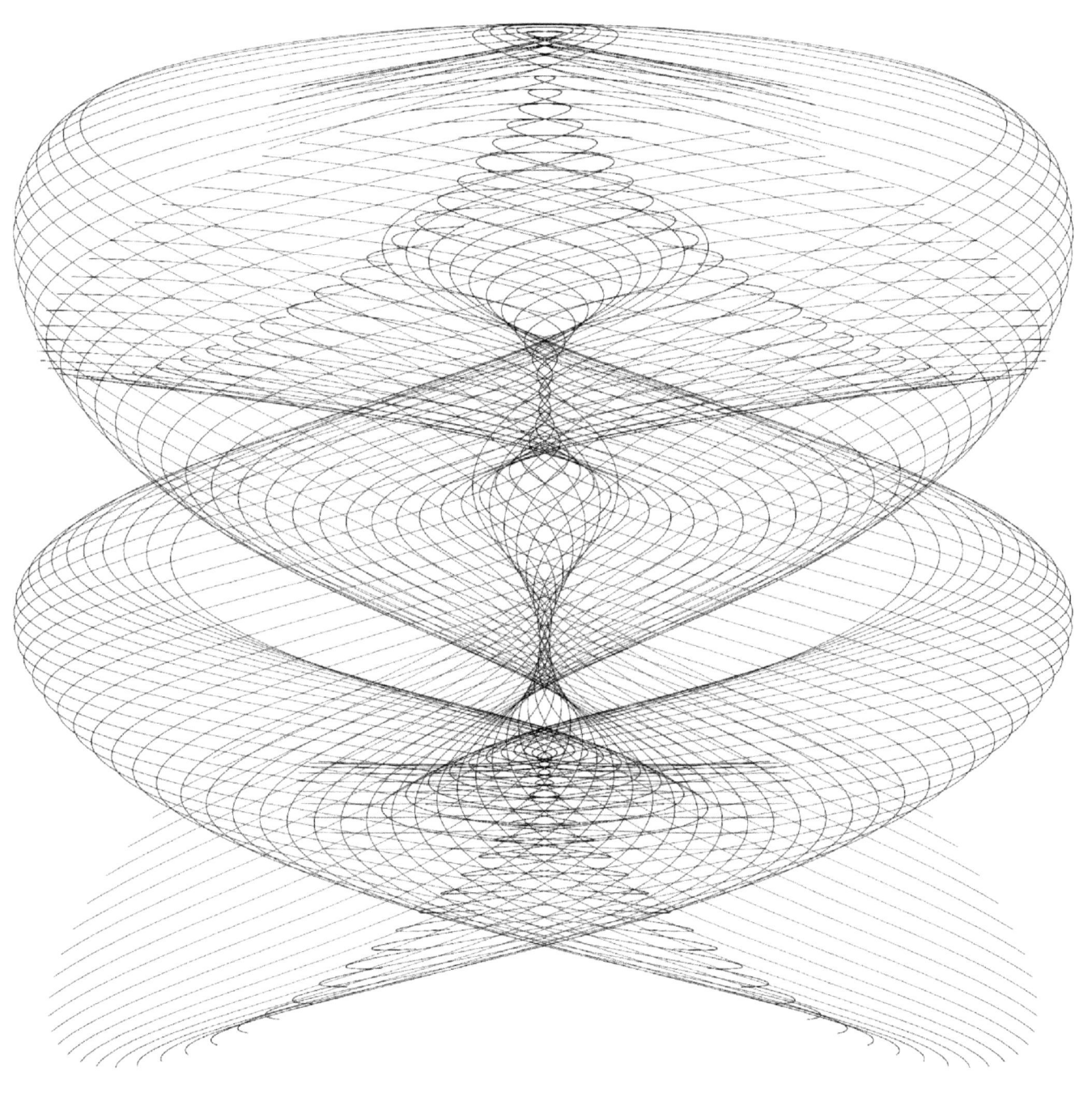

A warm smile is the universal language of kindness.
William Arthur Ward

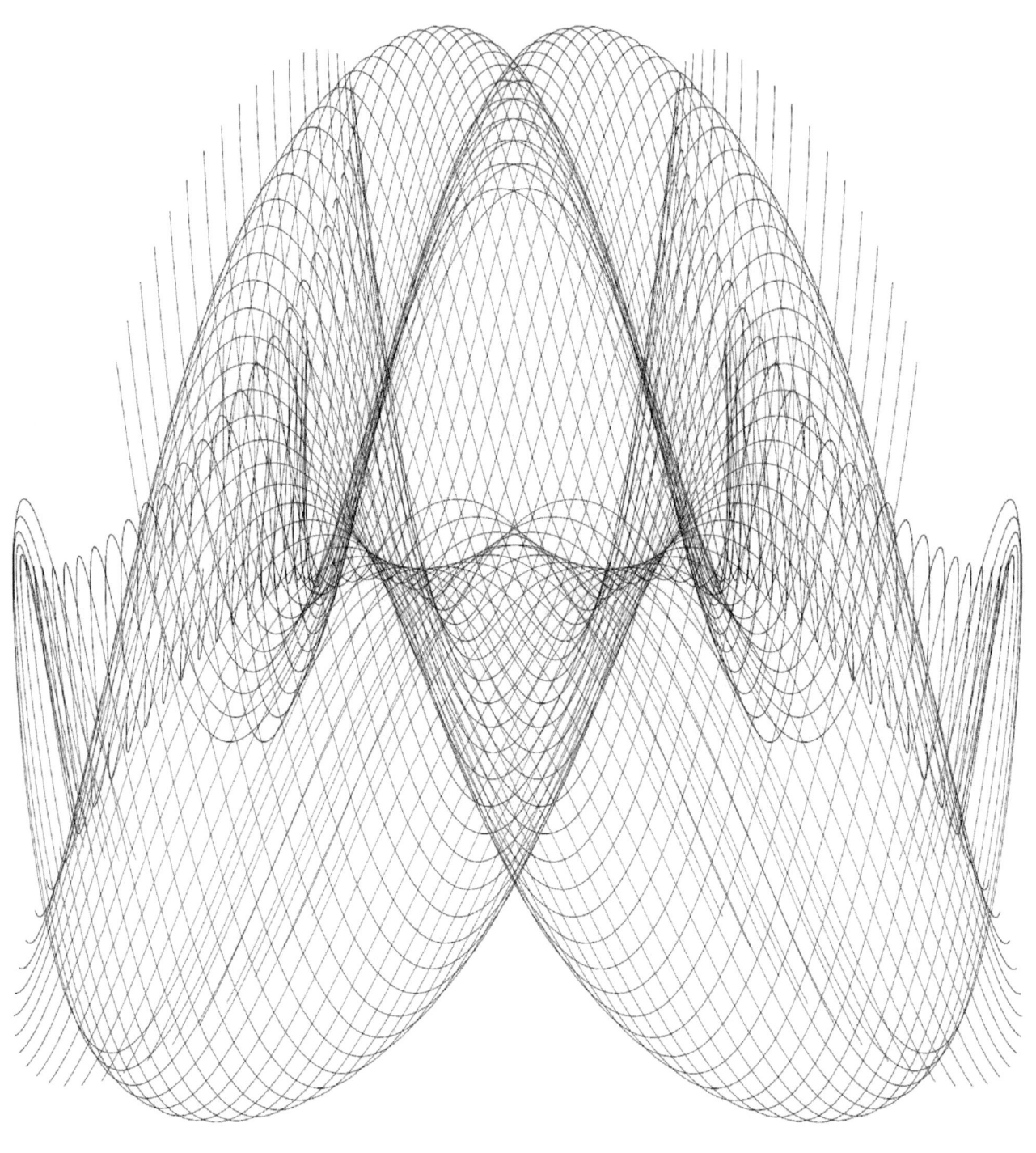

Be kind whenever possible.   It is always possible.
Dalai Lama

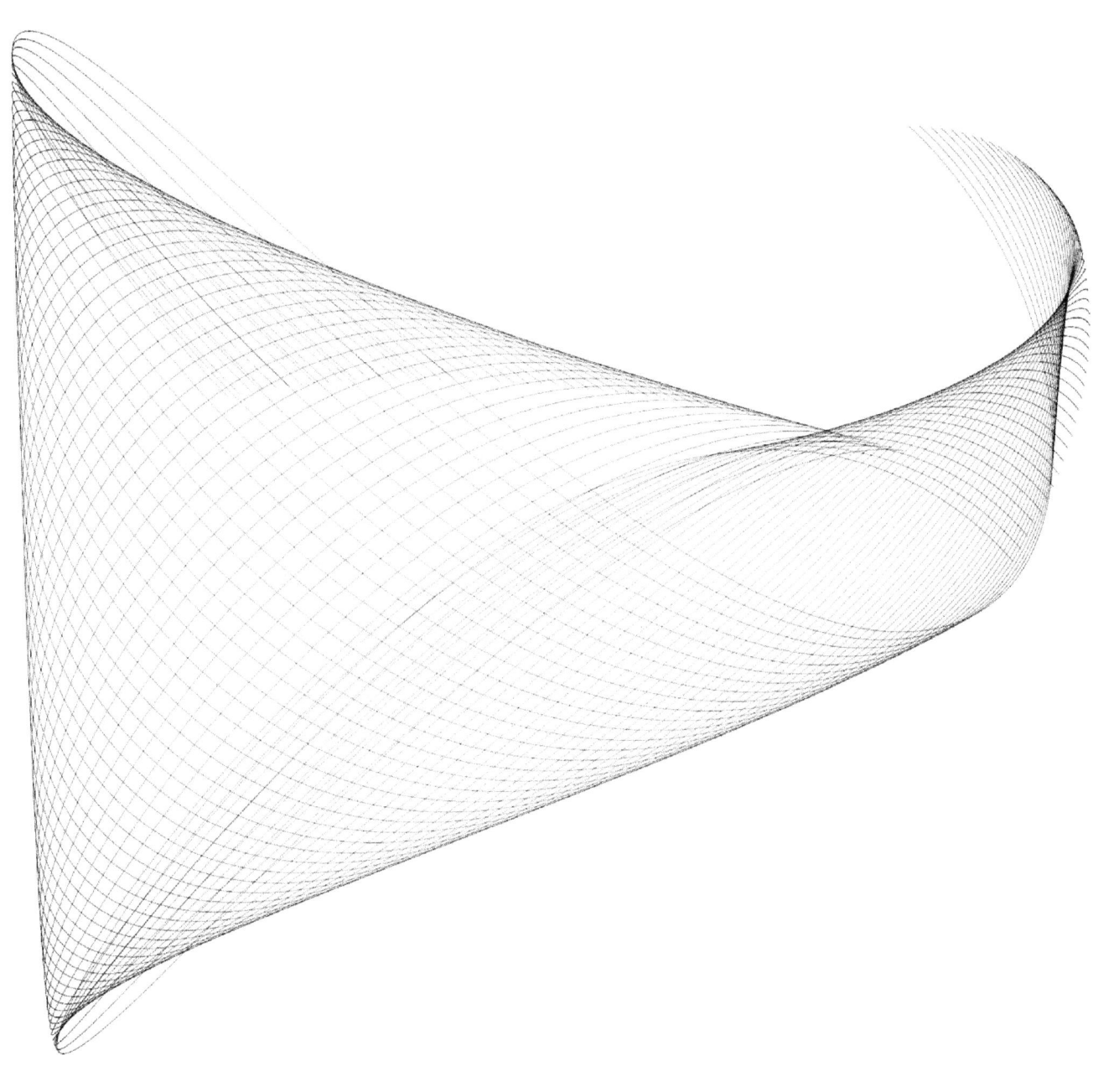

You only live once, but if you do it right, once is enough.
Mae West

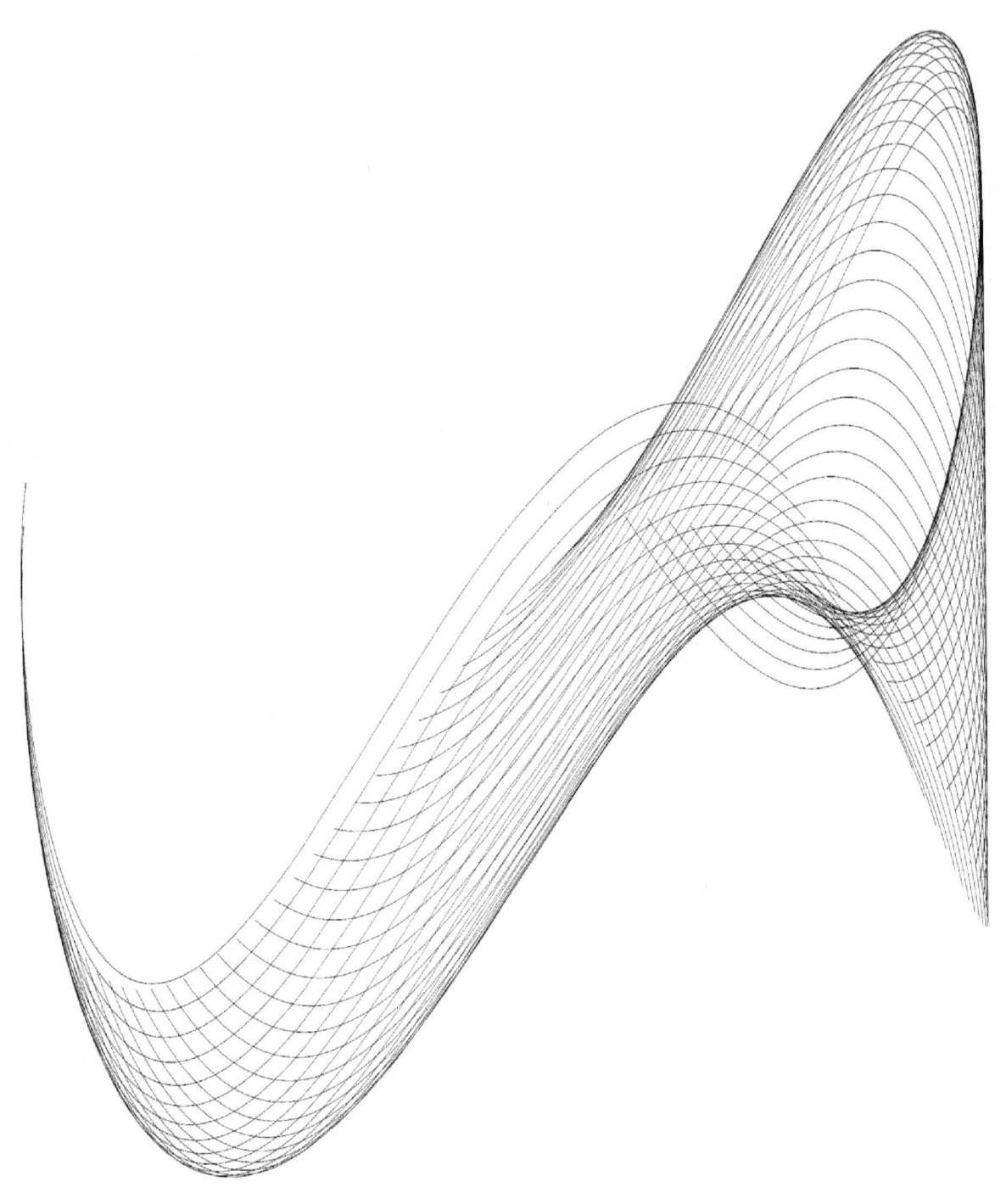

*It is better to be hated for
what you are than to be loved for what you are not.
André Gide*

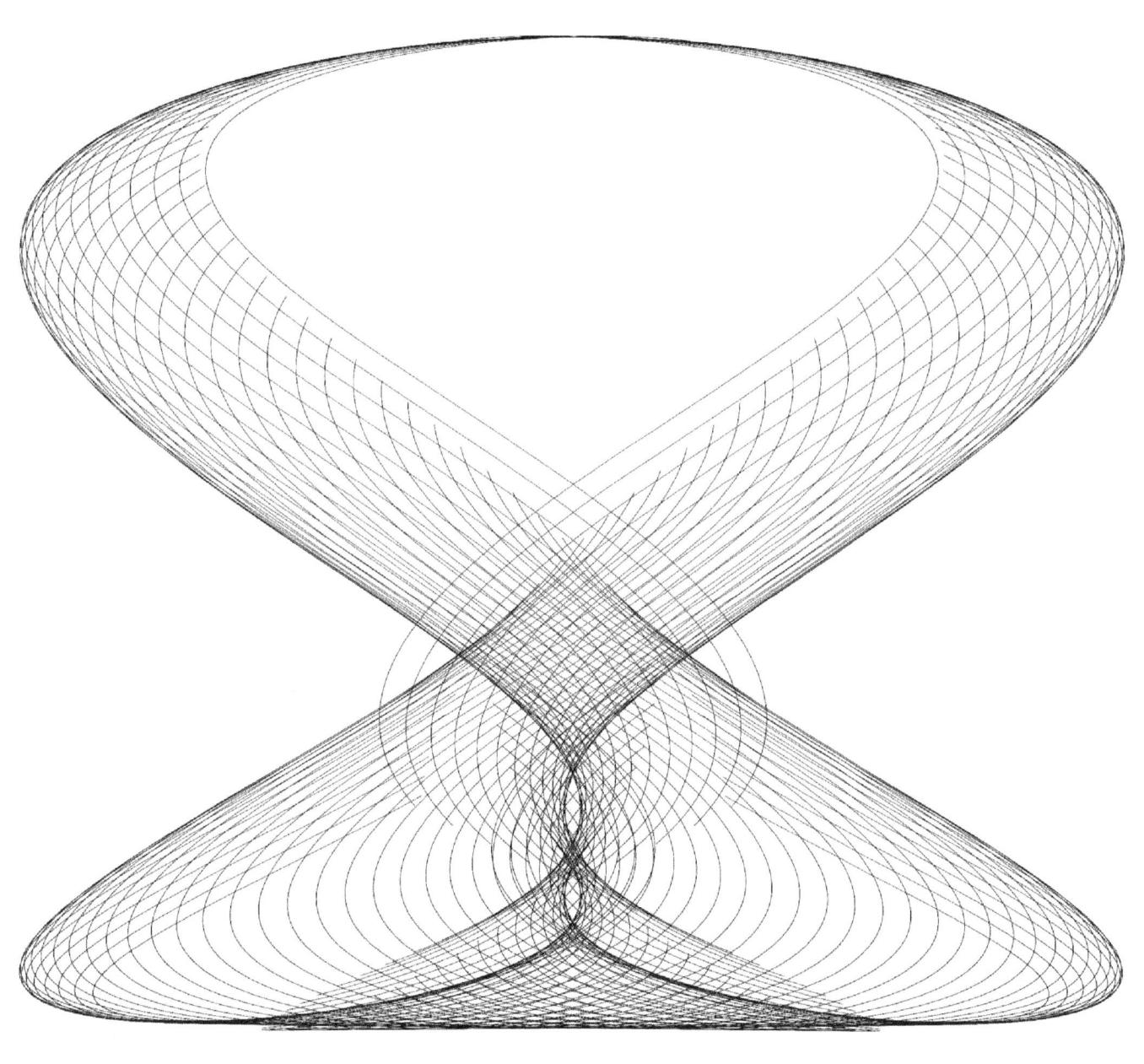

It does not do to dwell on dreams and forget to live.
J. K. Rowling

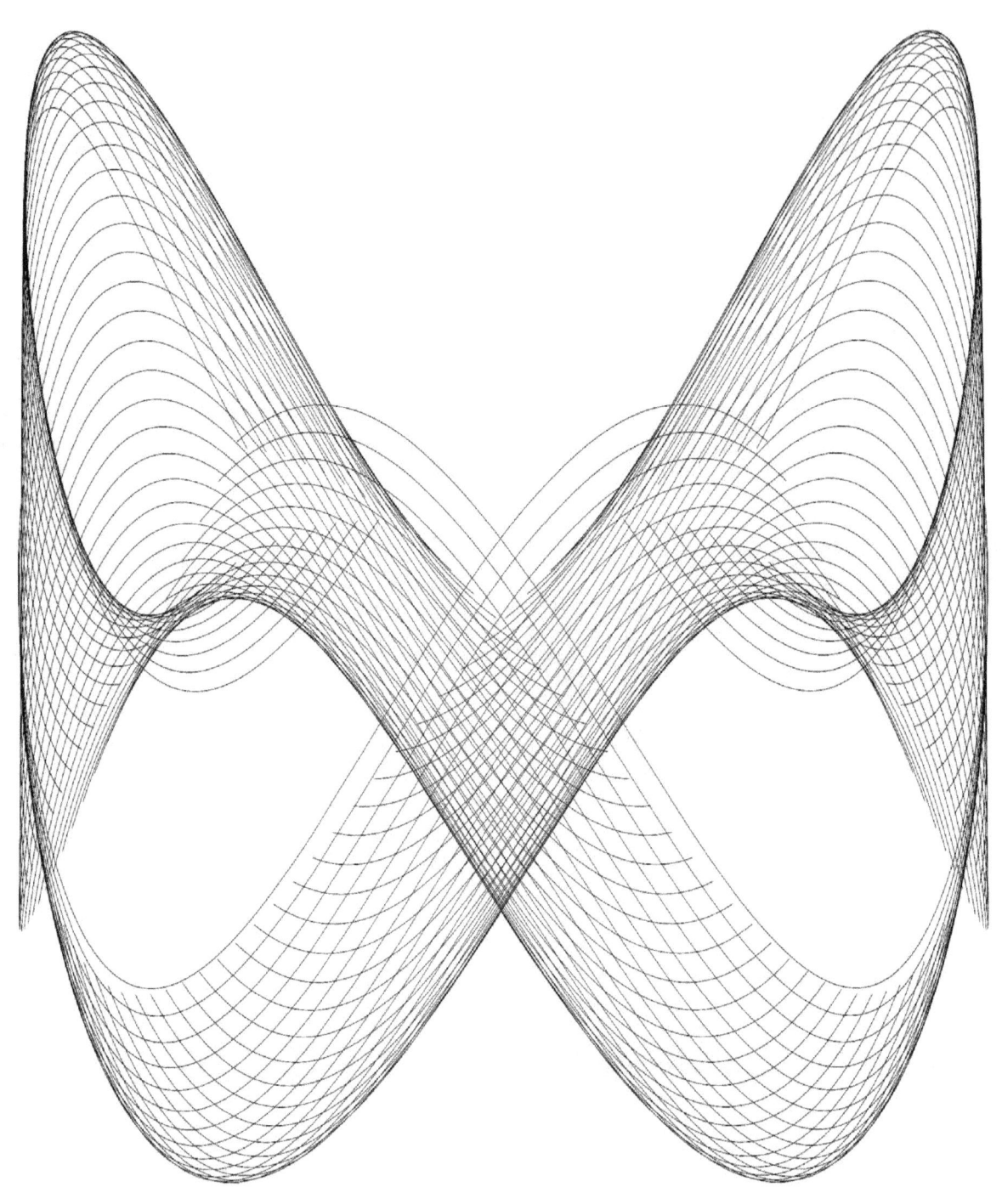

Everything you can imagine is real.
Pablo Picasso

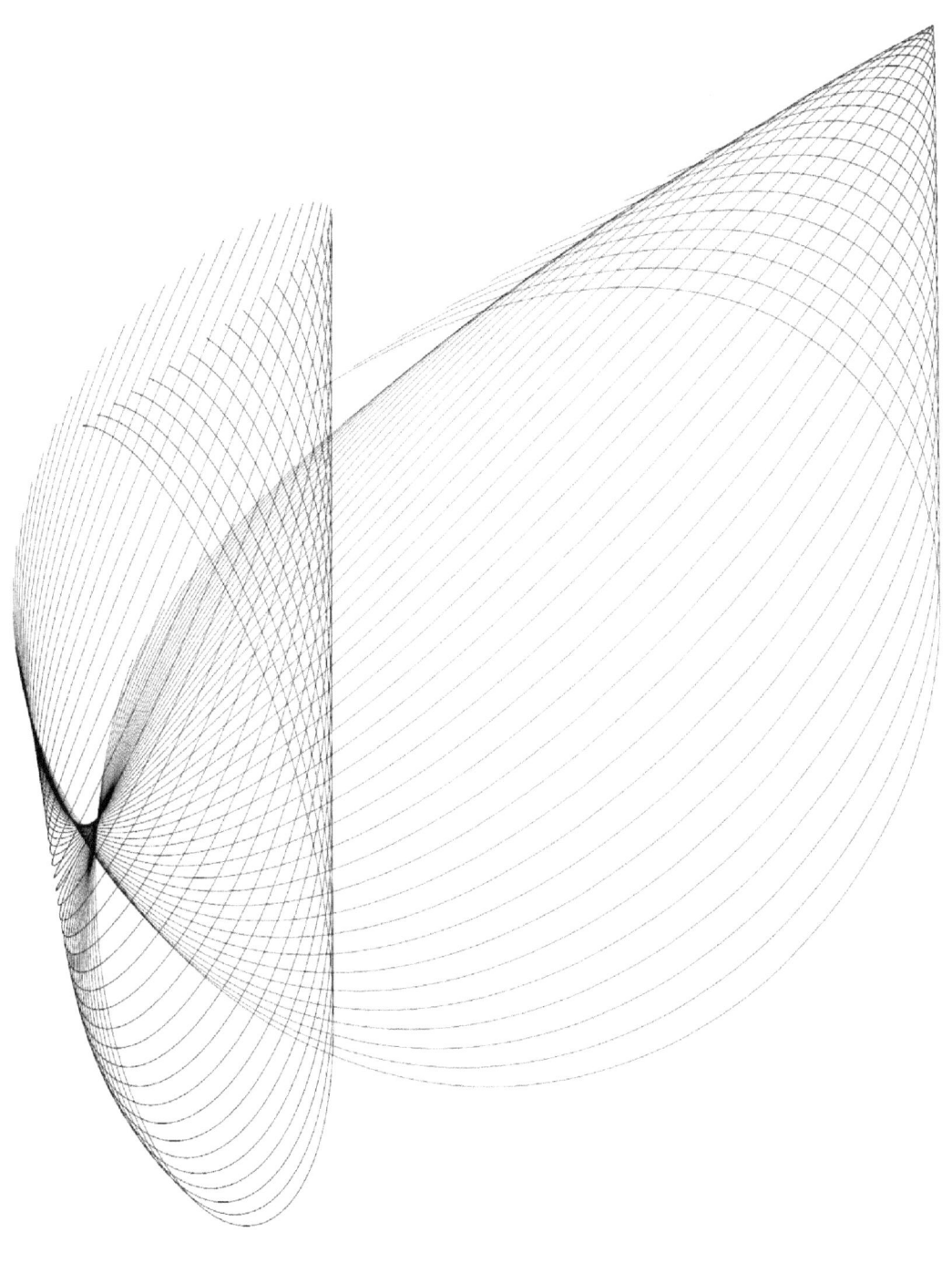

Life isn't about finding yourself. Life is about creating yourself.
George Bernard Shaw

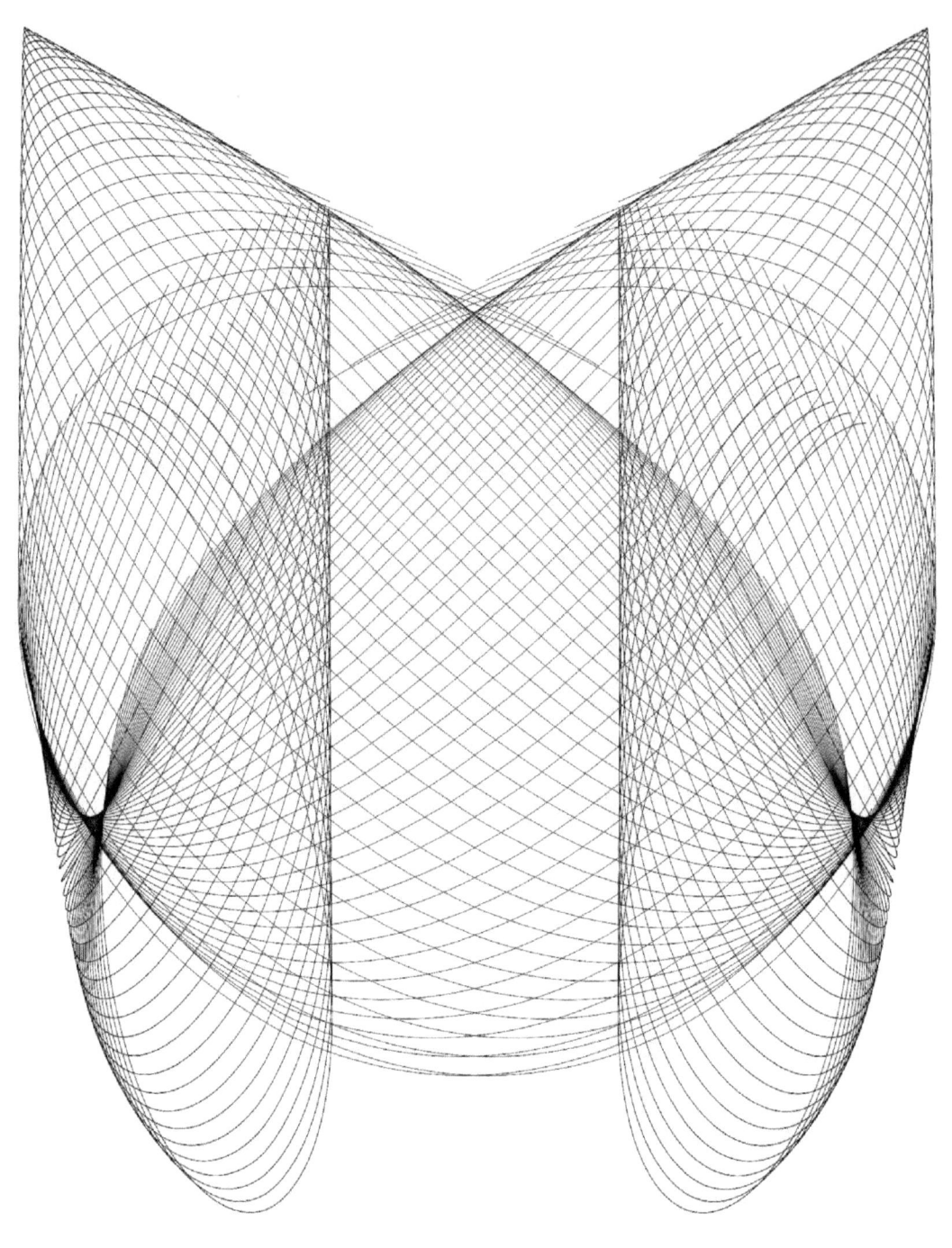

I like the night. Without the dark, we'd never see the stars.
Stephenie Meyer

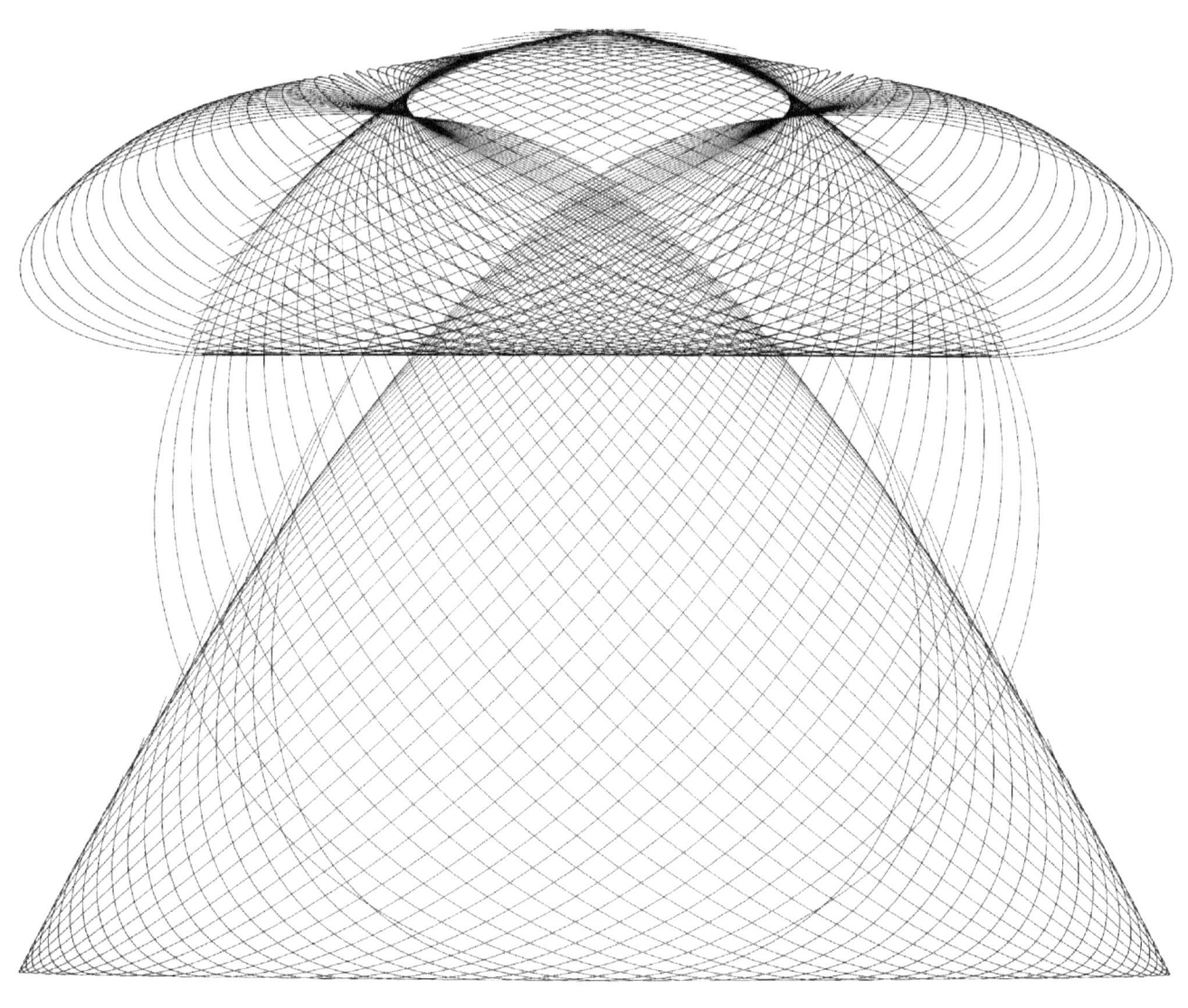

*Sometimes the dreams that come true
are the dreams you never even knew you had.
Alice Sebold*

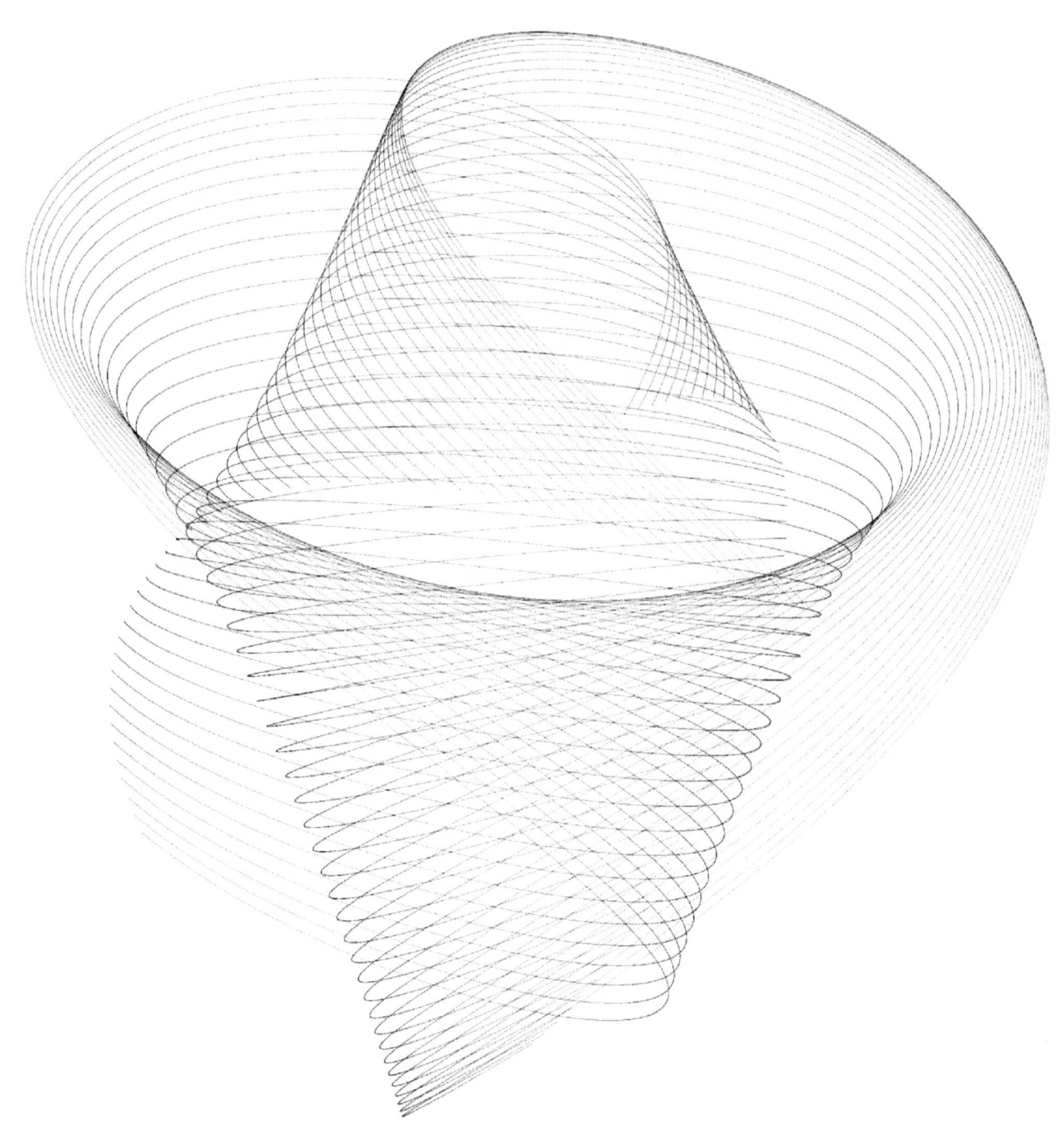

You're never given a dream
without also being given the power to make it true.
Richard Bach

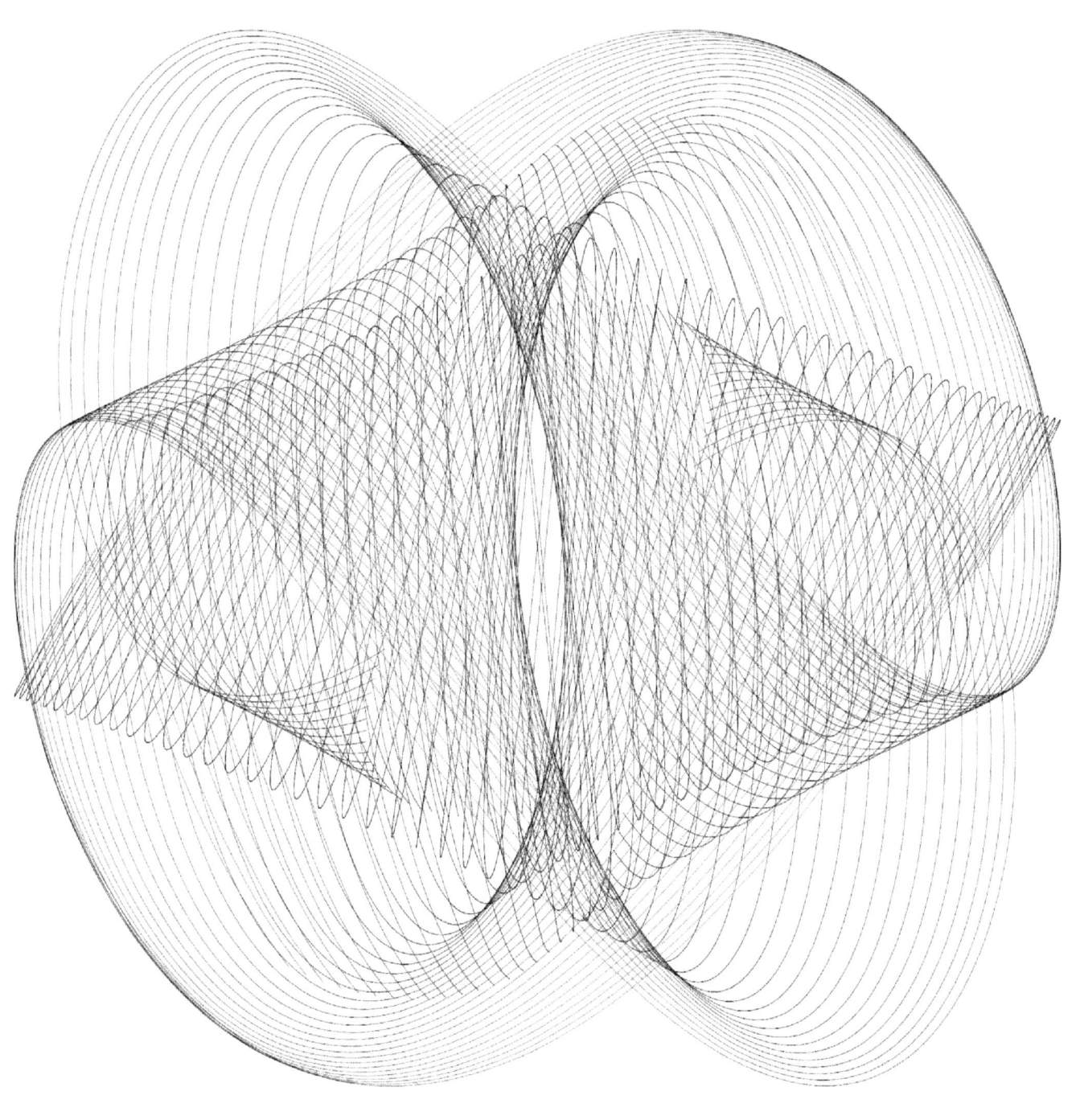

You yourself, as much as anybody in the entire universe,
deserve your love and affection
Gautama Buddha

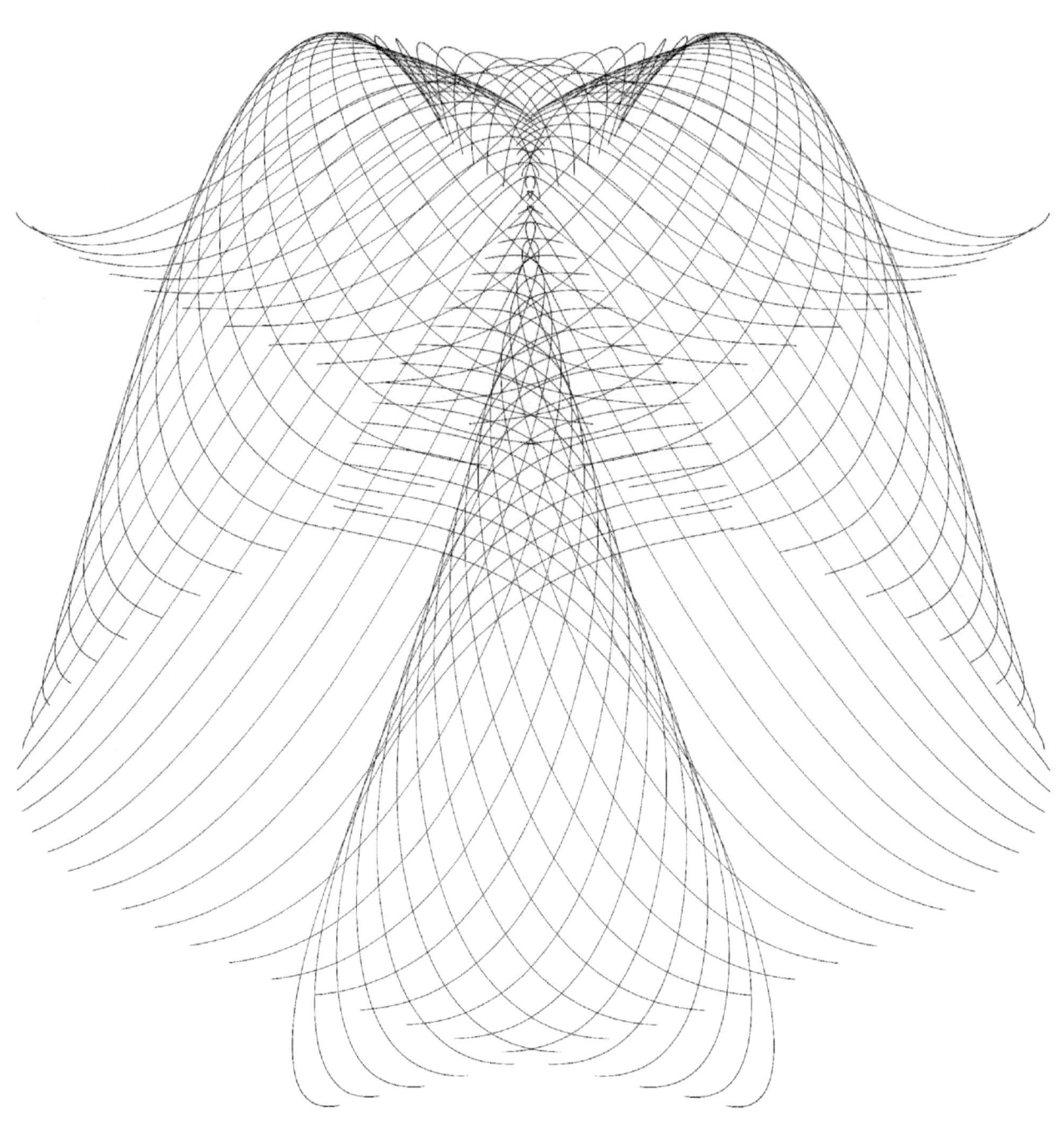

The only person who can pull me down is myself,
and I'm not going to let myself pull me down anymore.
C. JoyBell C.

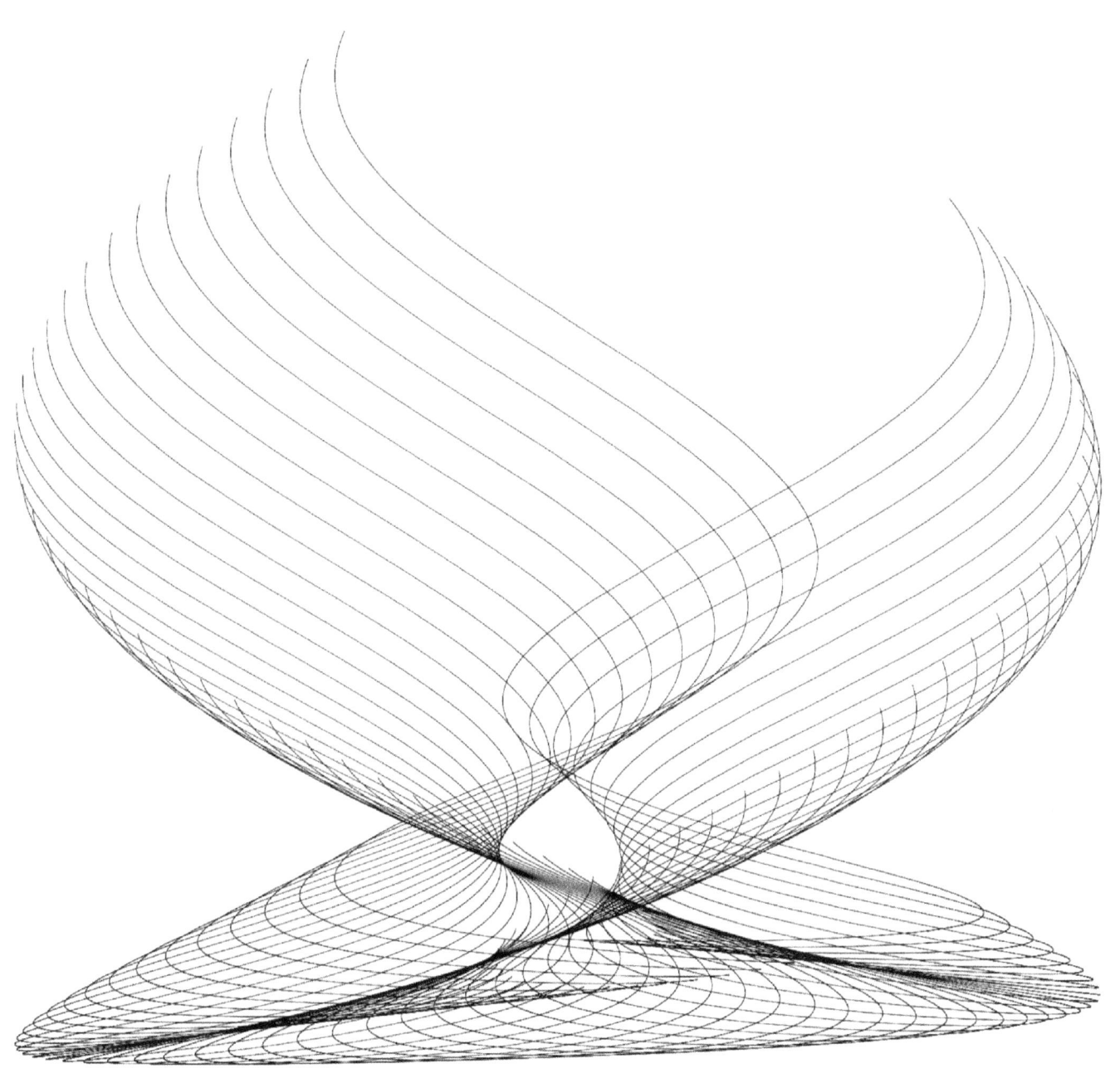

With the new day comes new strength and new thoughts.
Eleanor Roosevelt

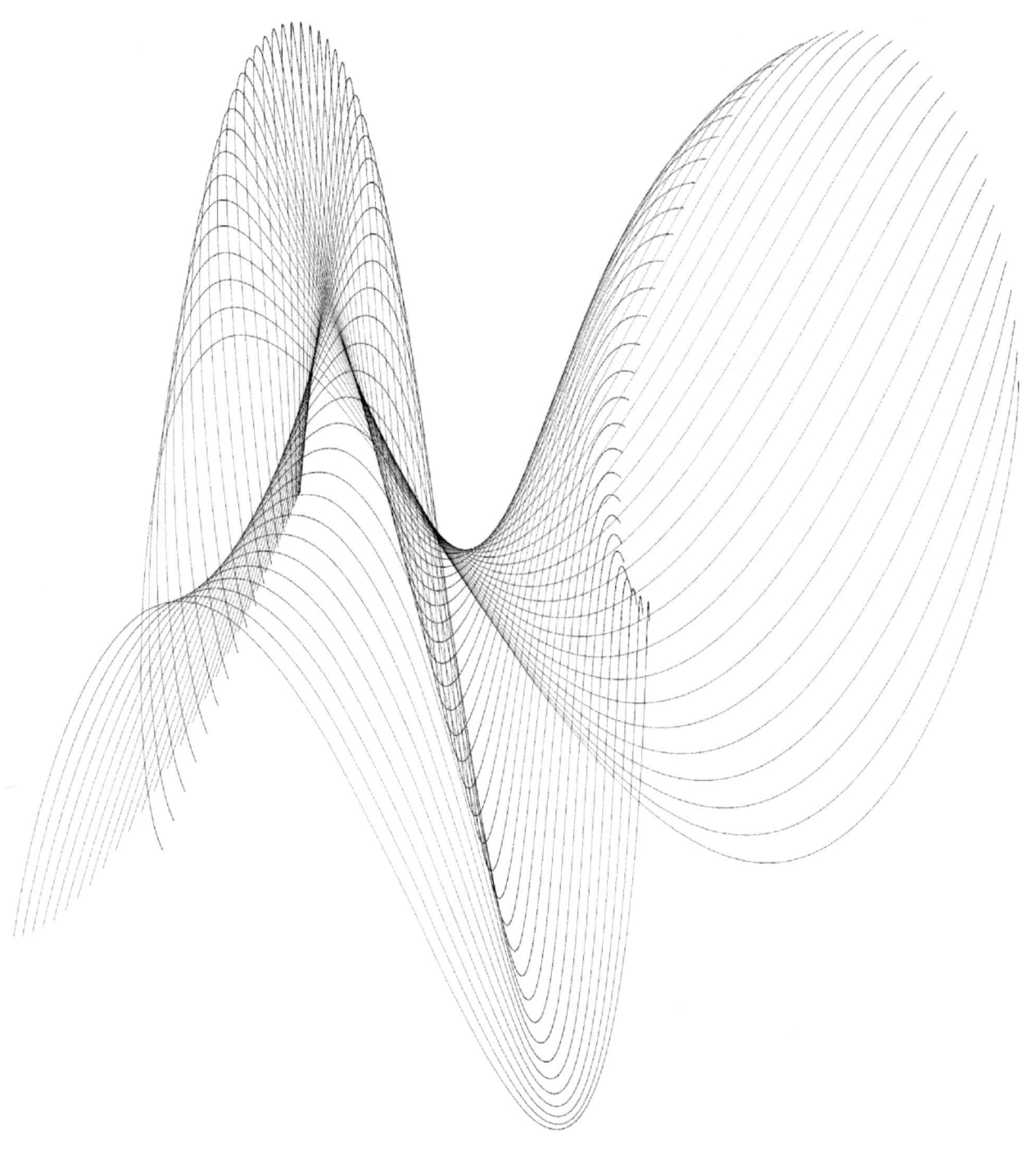

When you're at the end of your rope, tie a knot and hold on.
Theodore Roosevelt

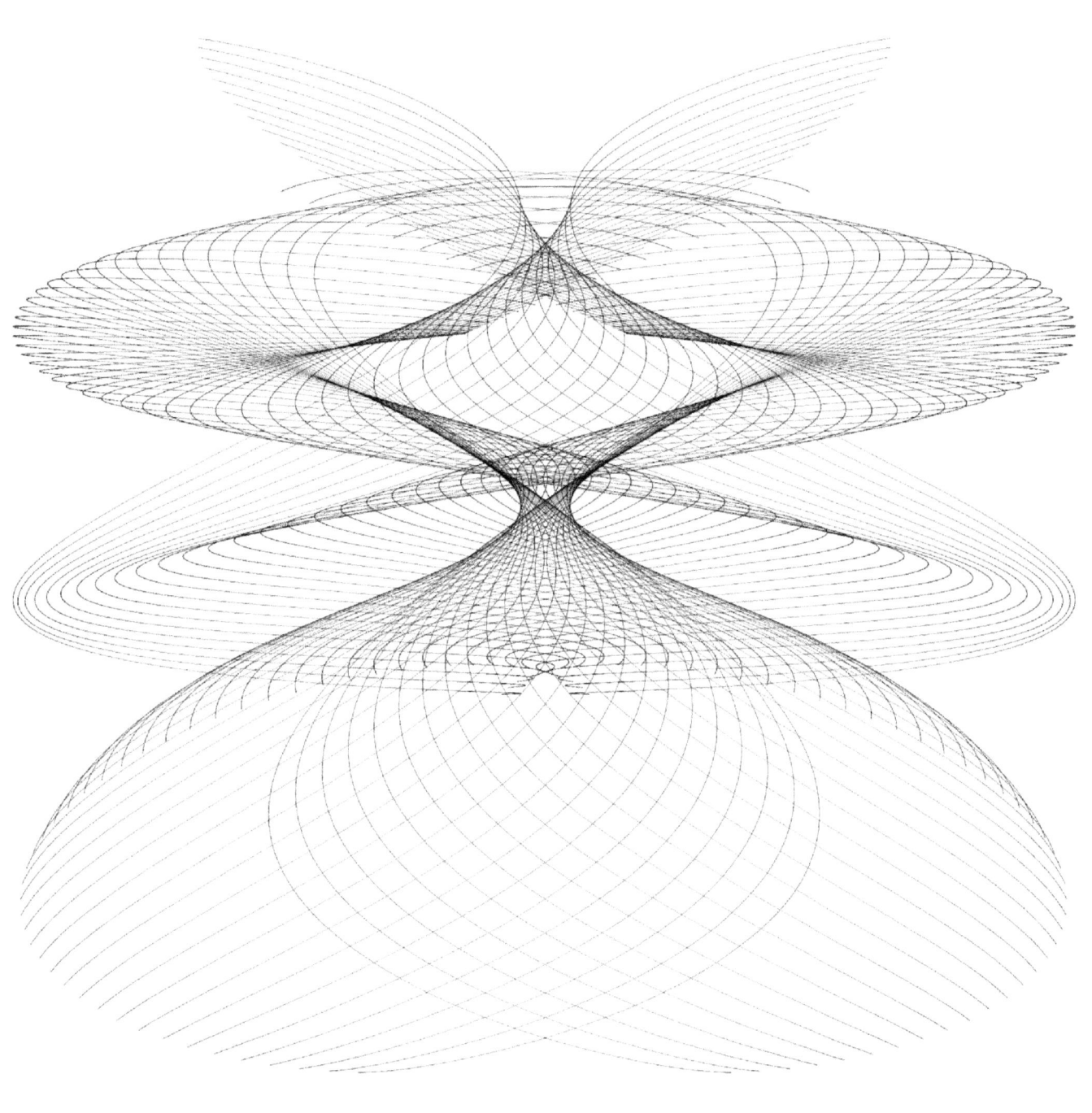

Imagination is the highest form of research.
Albert Einstein

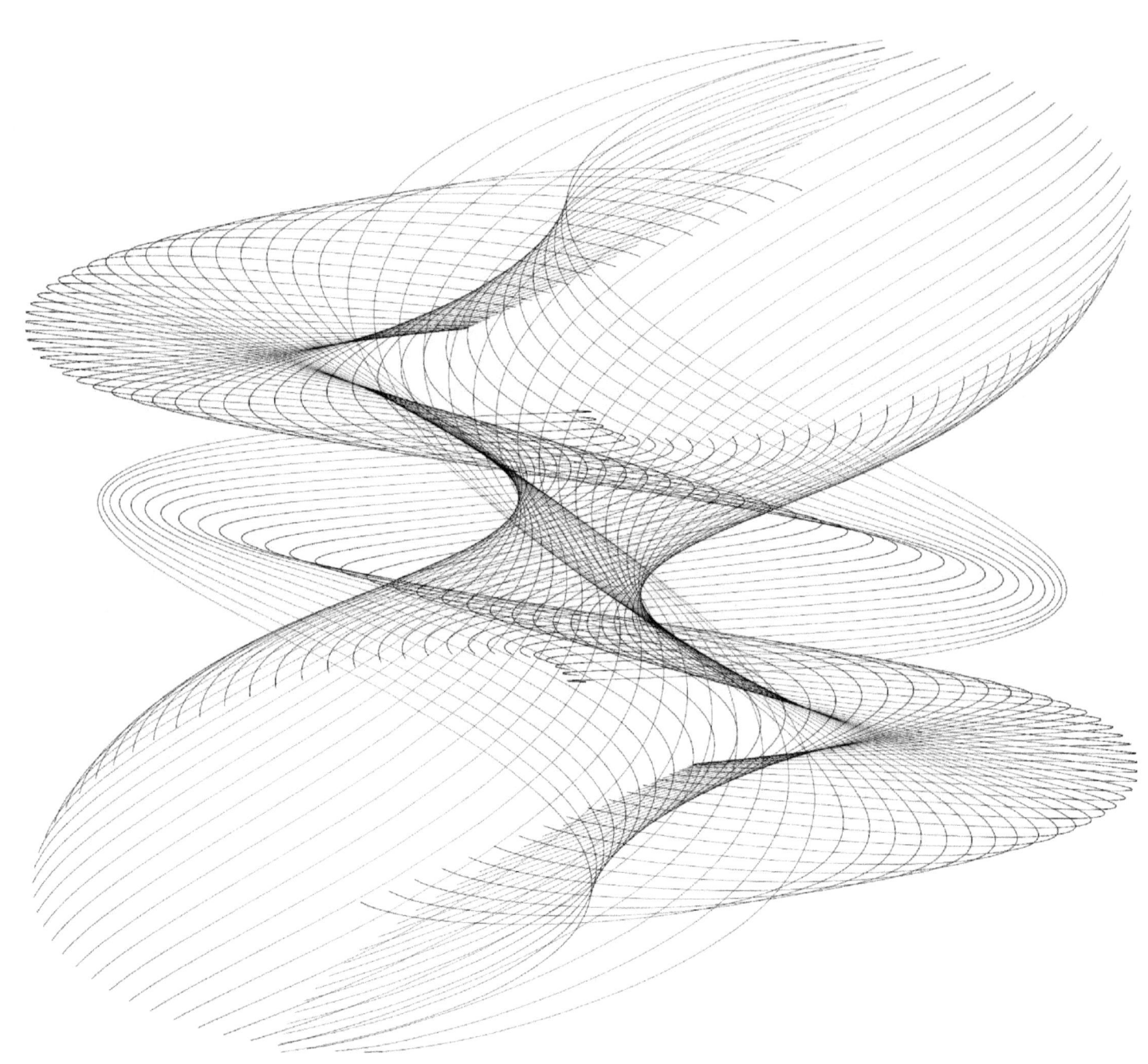

You must not ever stop being whimsical.
And you must not, ever, give anyone else the responsibility for your life.
Mary Oliver

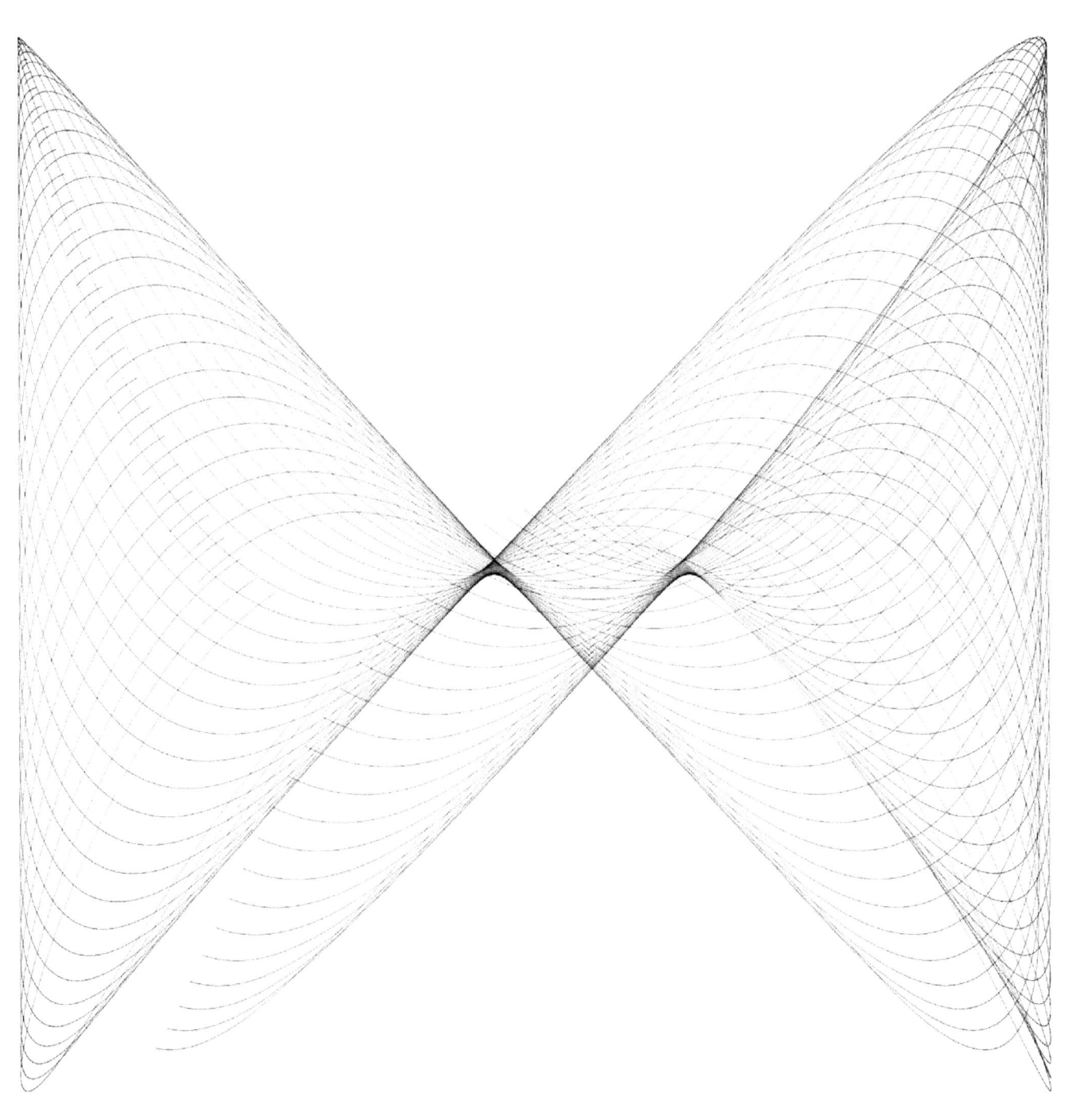

You must give everything to make your life
as beautiful as the dreams that dance in your imagination.
Roman Payne

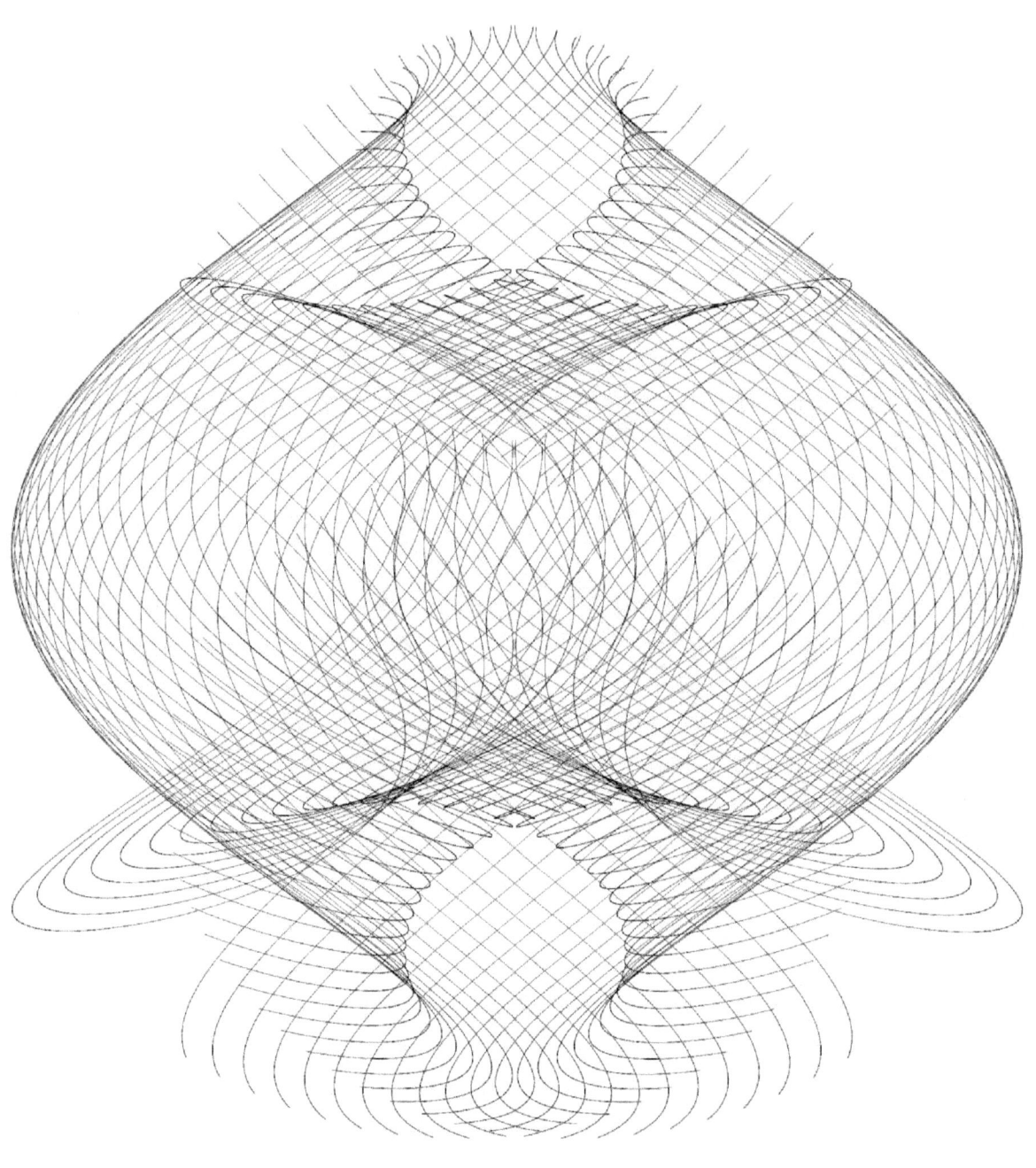

Don't tell me the sky's the limit when there are footprints on the moon.
Paul Brandt

Obstacles are things a person sees when he takes his eyes off his goal.
E. Joseph Cossman

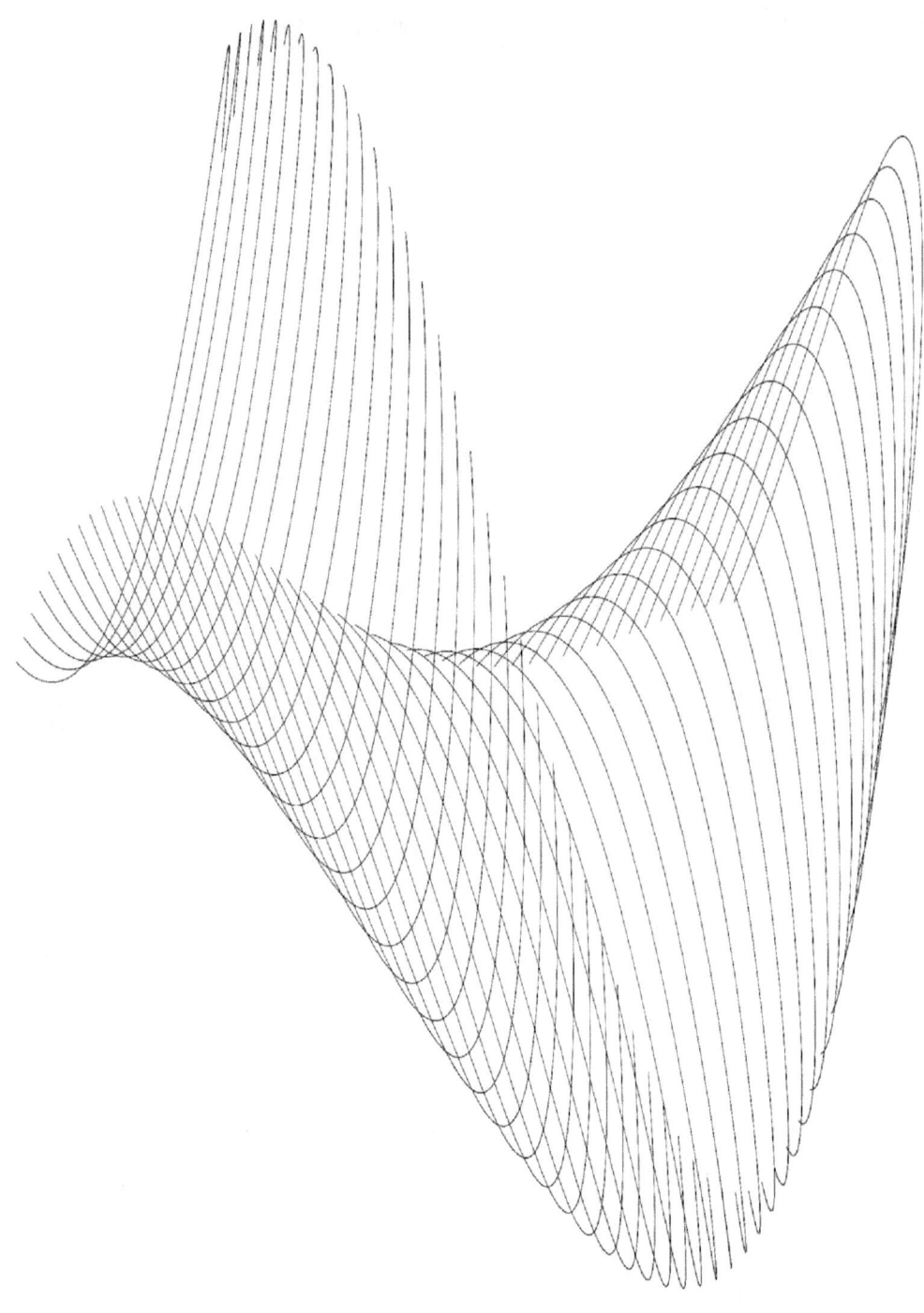

The difference between you and everyone else, is everyone else.
And that's a lot, so you should feel special.
Jarod Kintz

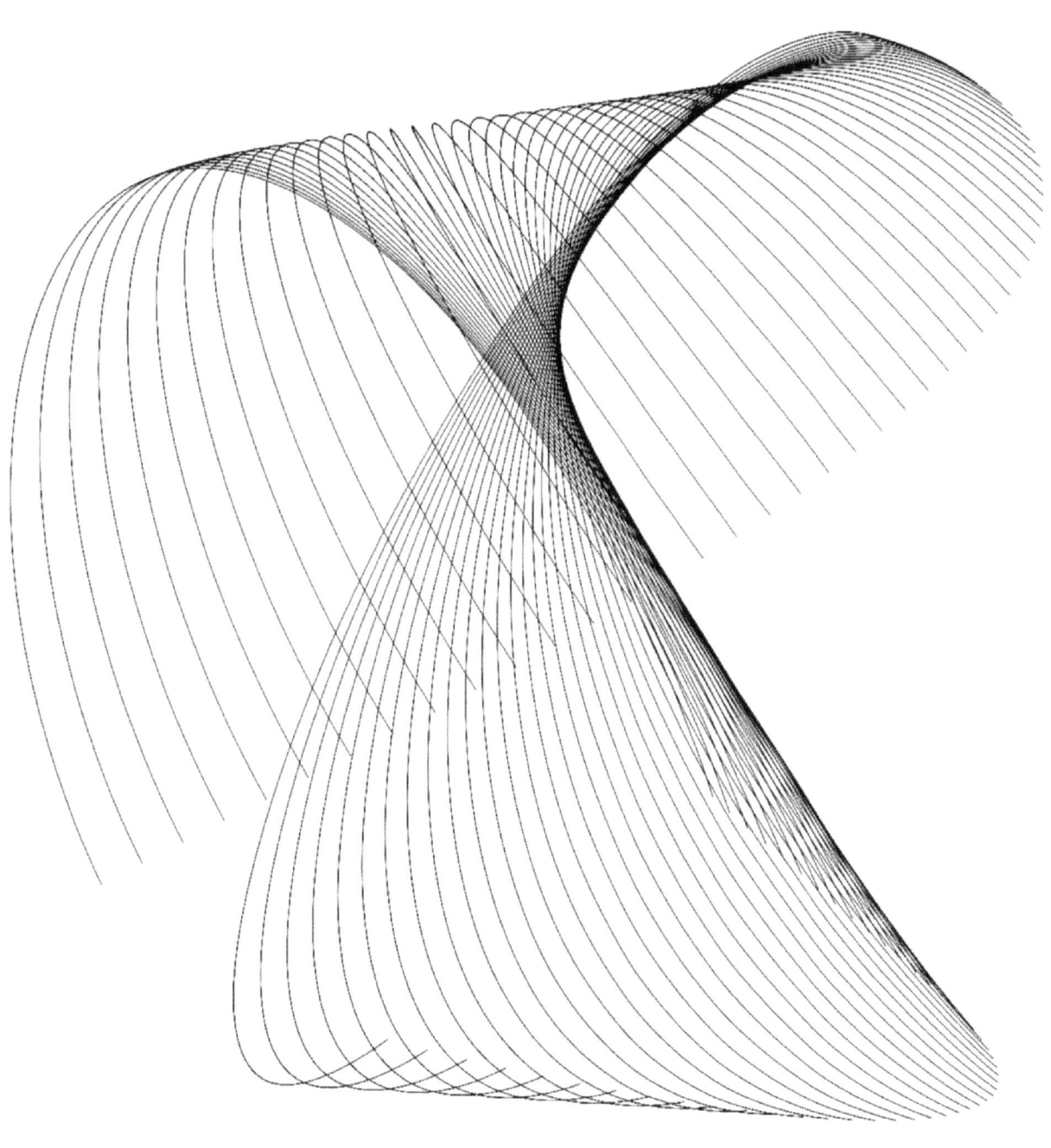

Head up, heart open. To better days!
T. F. Hodge

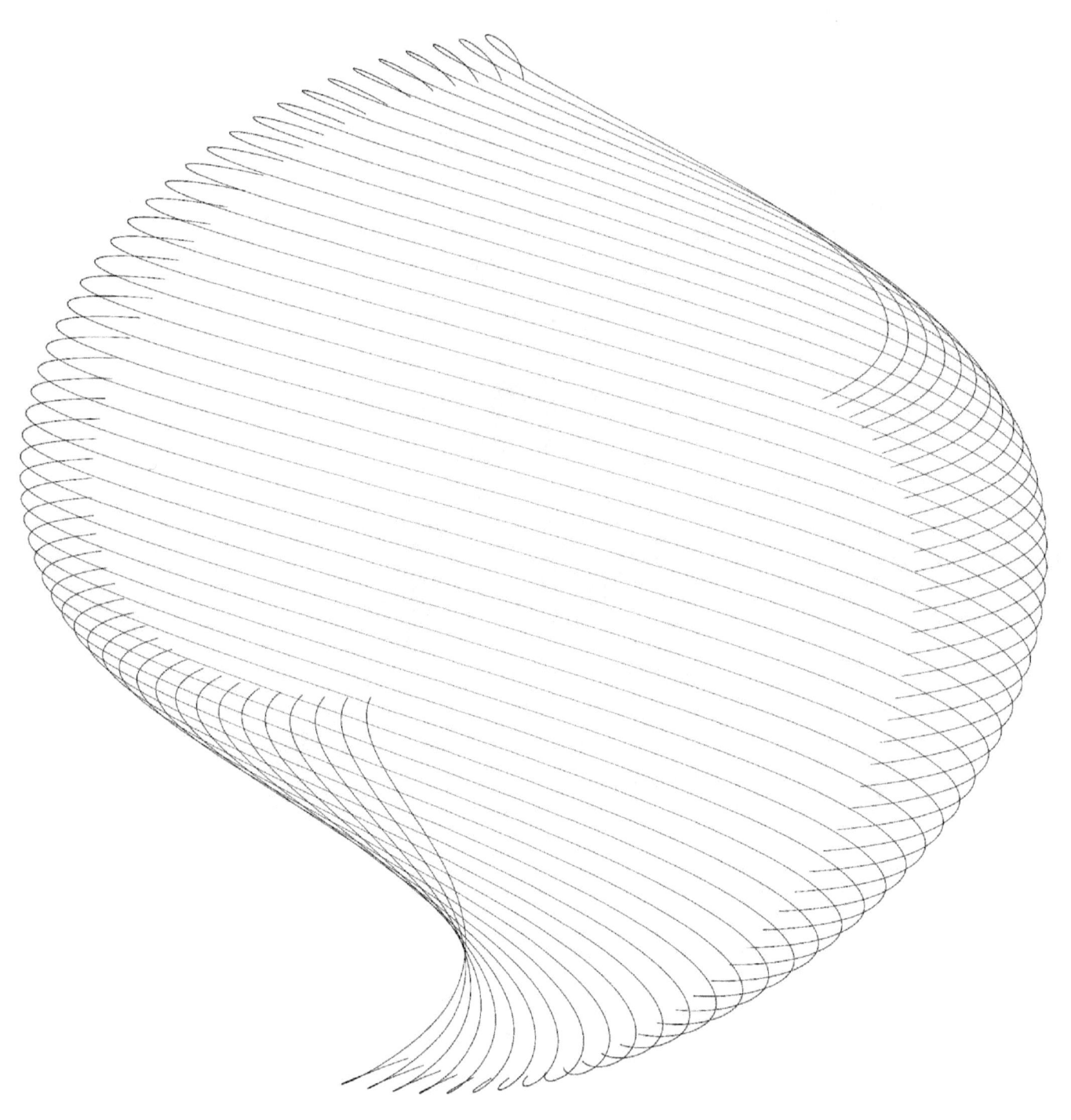

Everything you need to know
you have learned through your journey.
Paulo Coelho

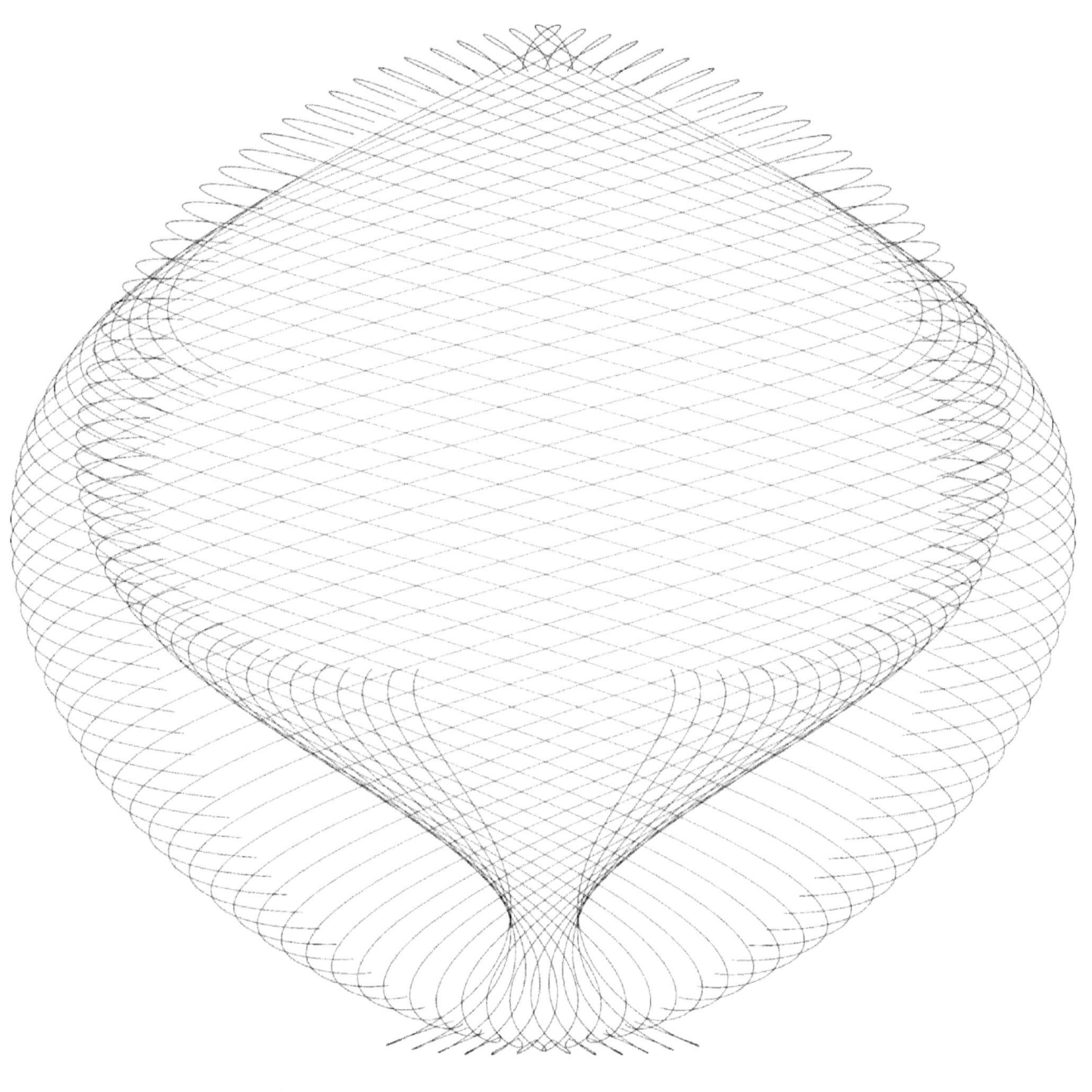

Sorrow looks back. Worry looks around. Faith looks up
Ralph Waldo Emerson

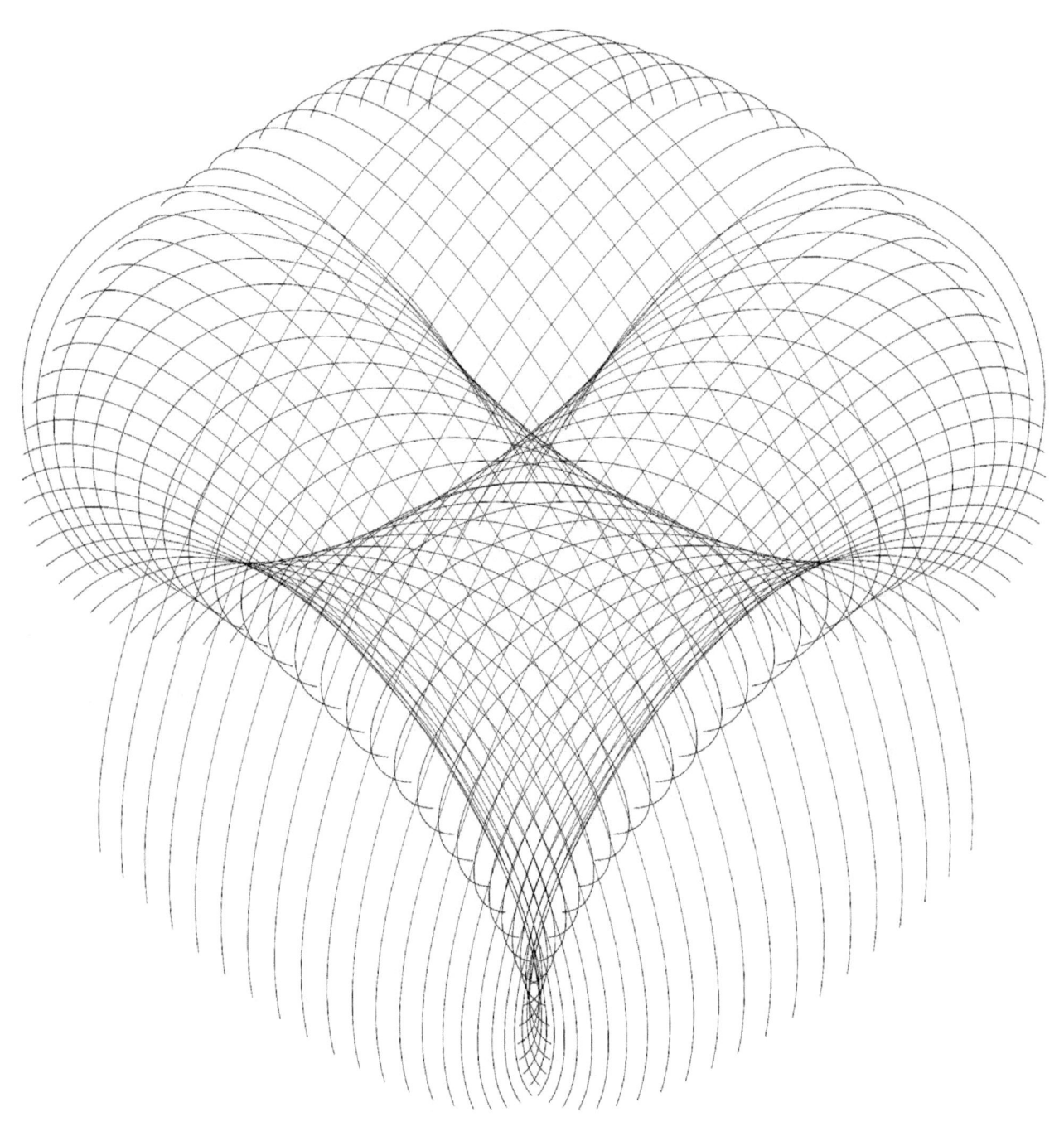

If you can't fight and you can't flee, flow.
Robert Elias

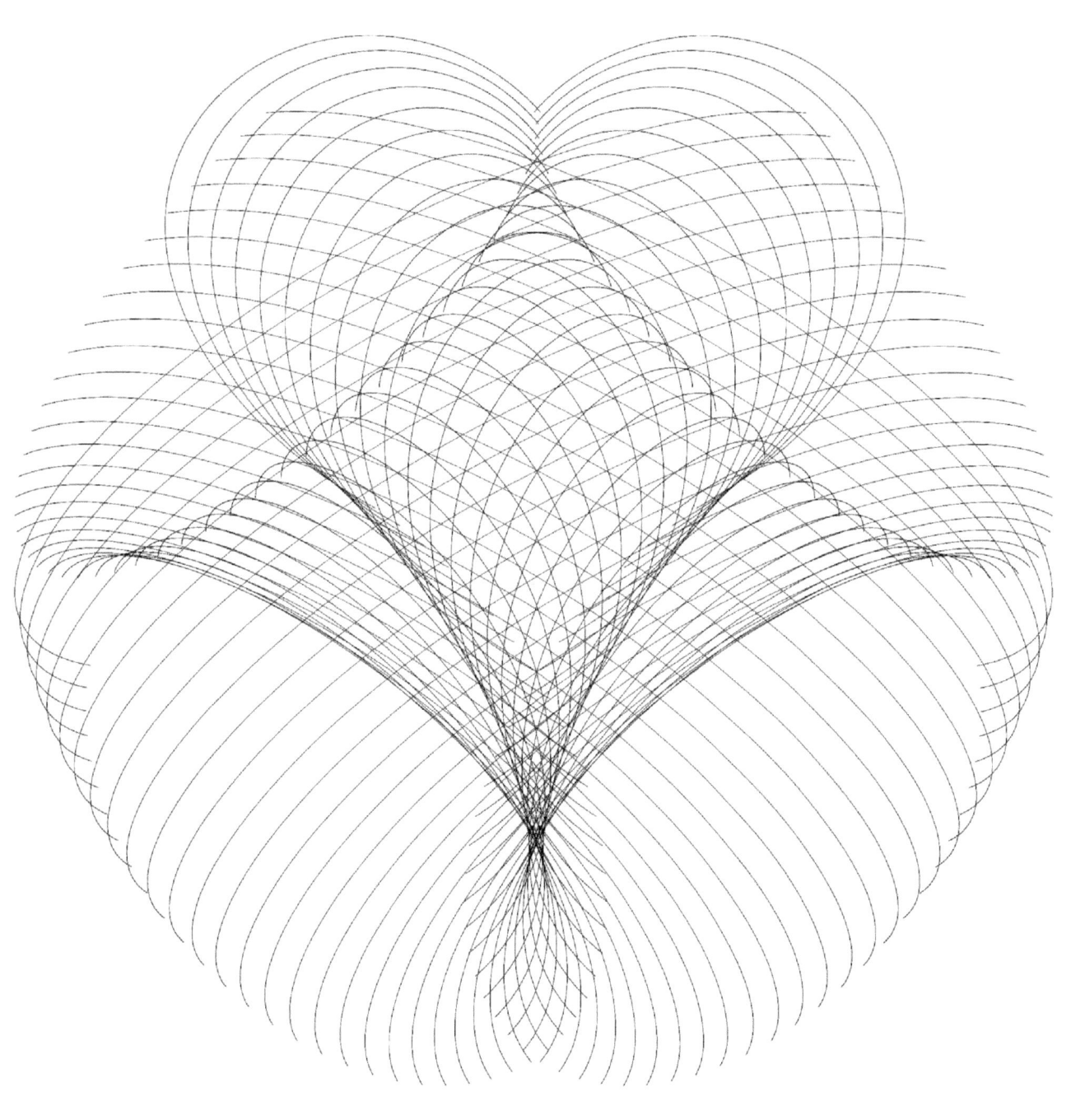

Life doesn't require that we be the best, only that we try our best.
H. Jackson Brown Jr.

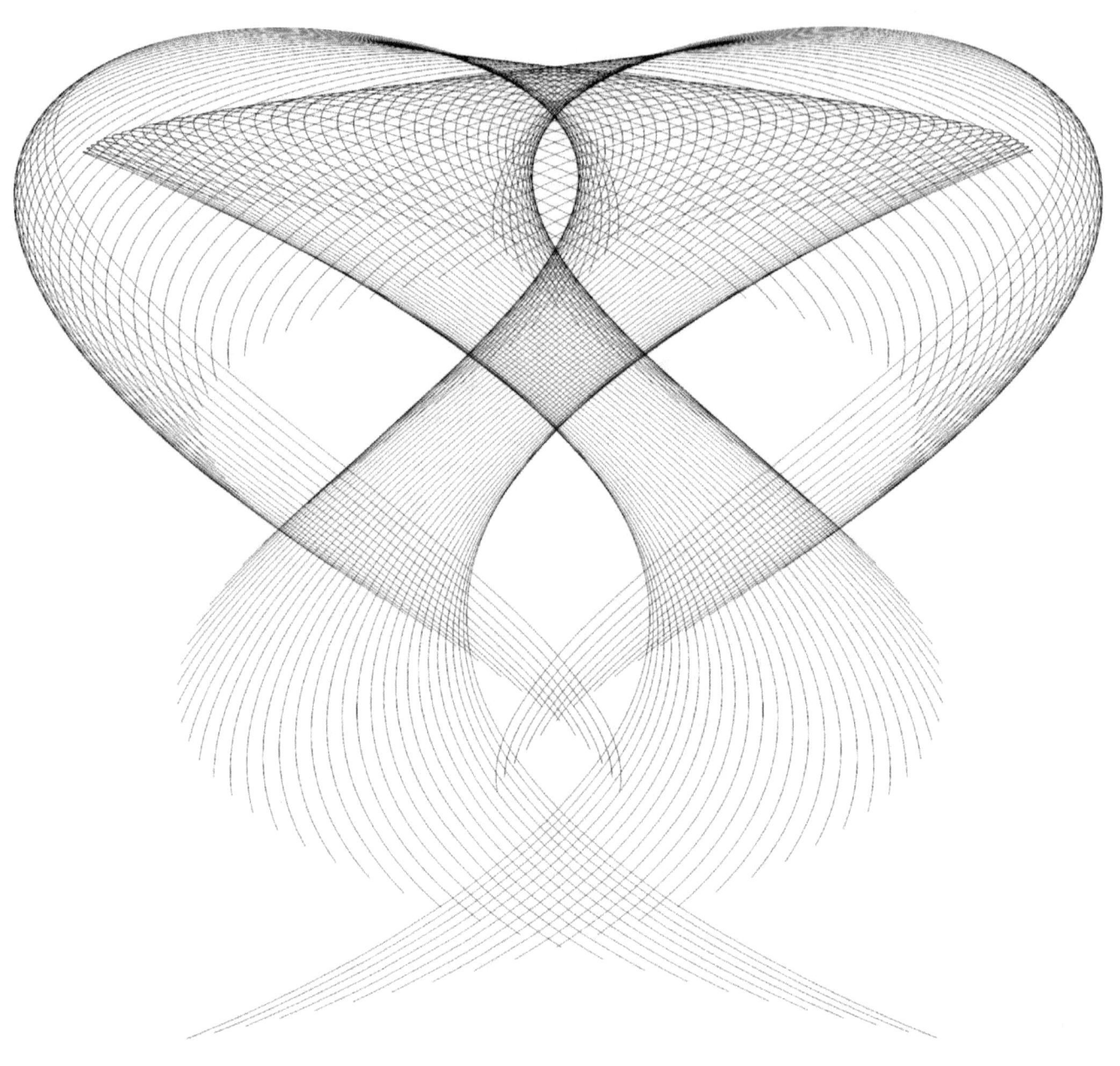

Only those who look with the eyes of children
can lose themselves in the object of their wonder.
Eberhard Arnold

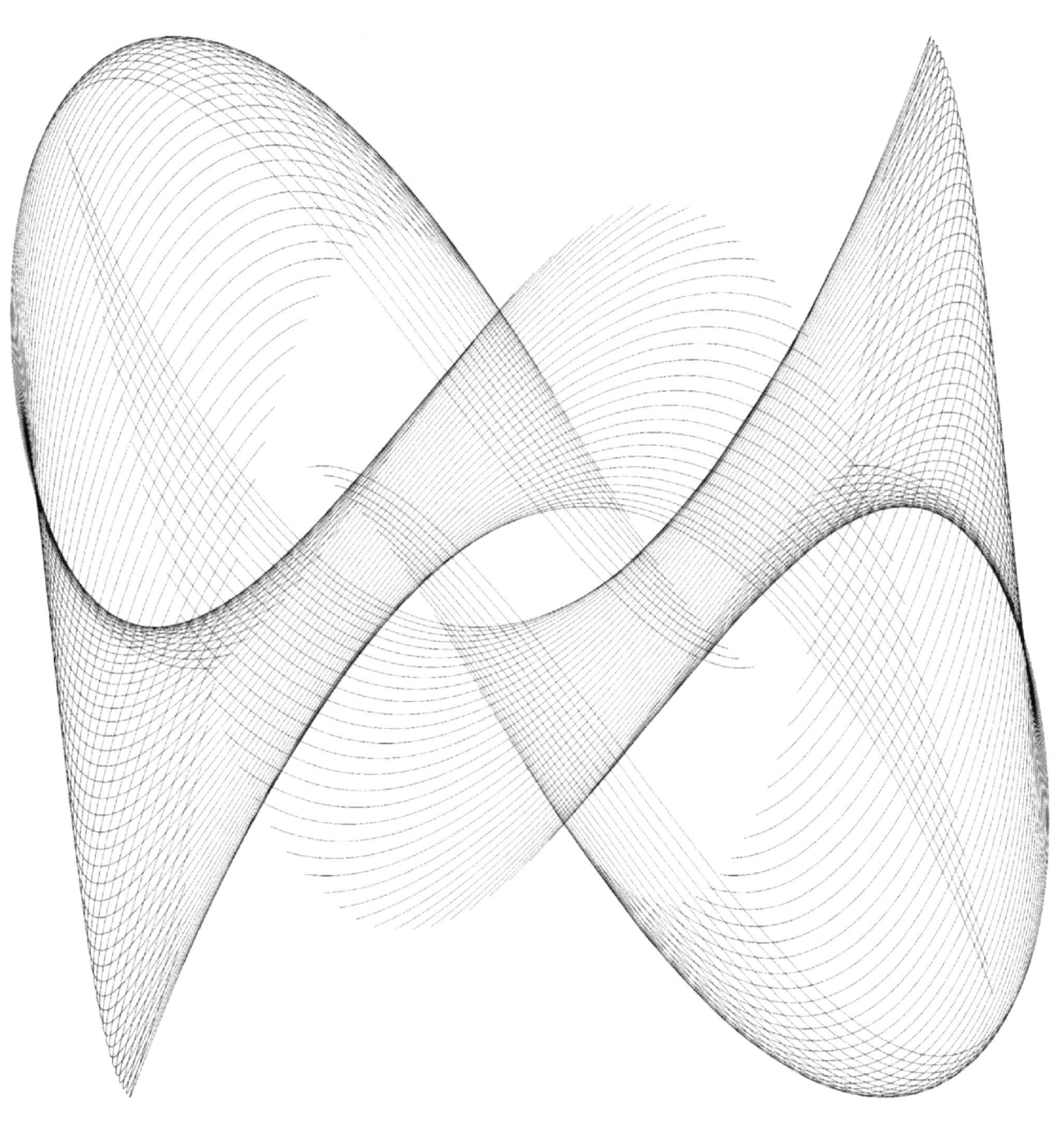

Don't set your goals by what other people deem important.
Jaachynma N. E. Agu

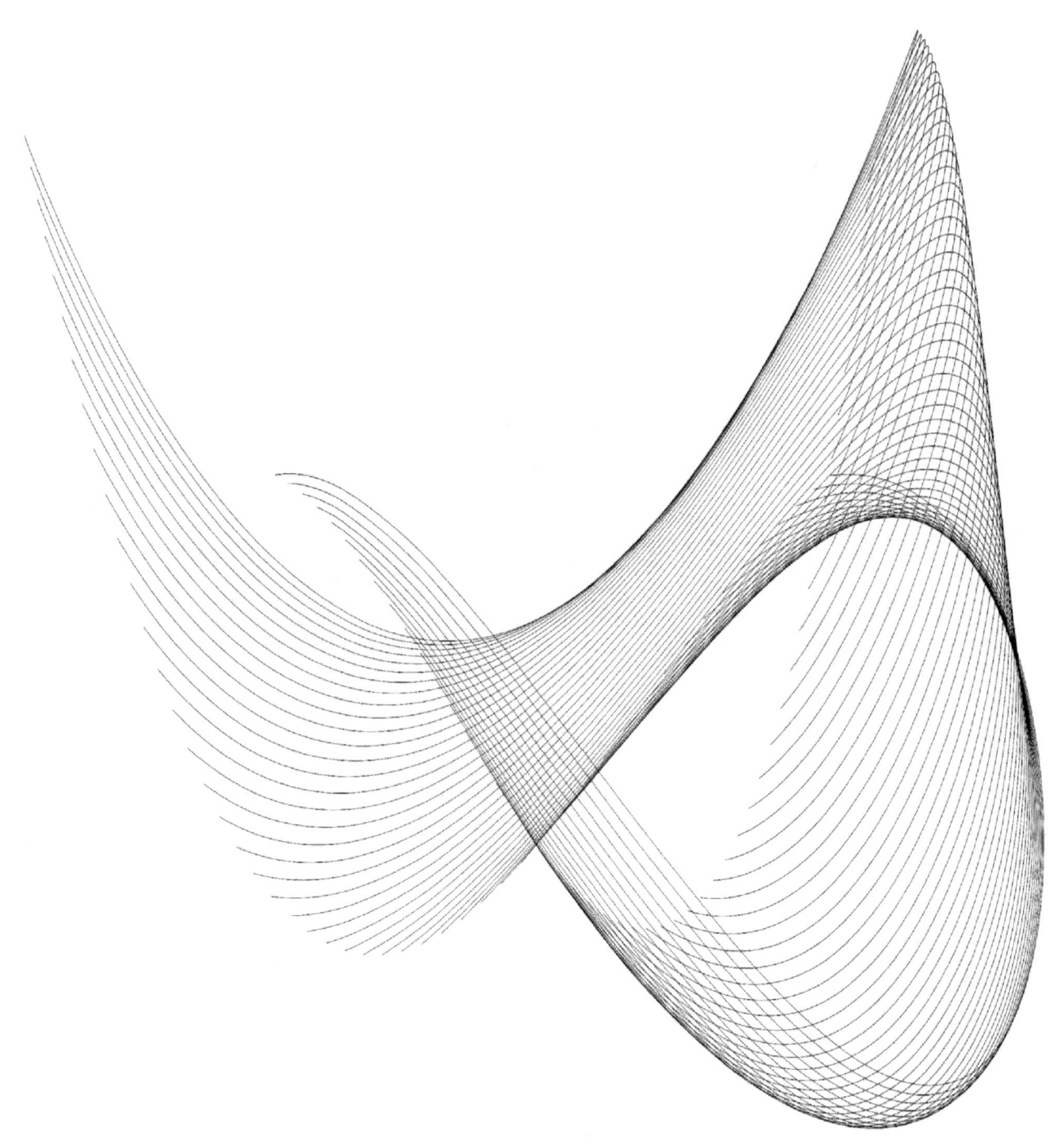

I must work harder to achieve my goal
of not seeking approval from those whose approval
I'm not even sure is important to me.
Lauren Graham

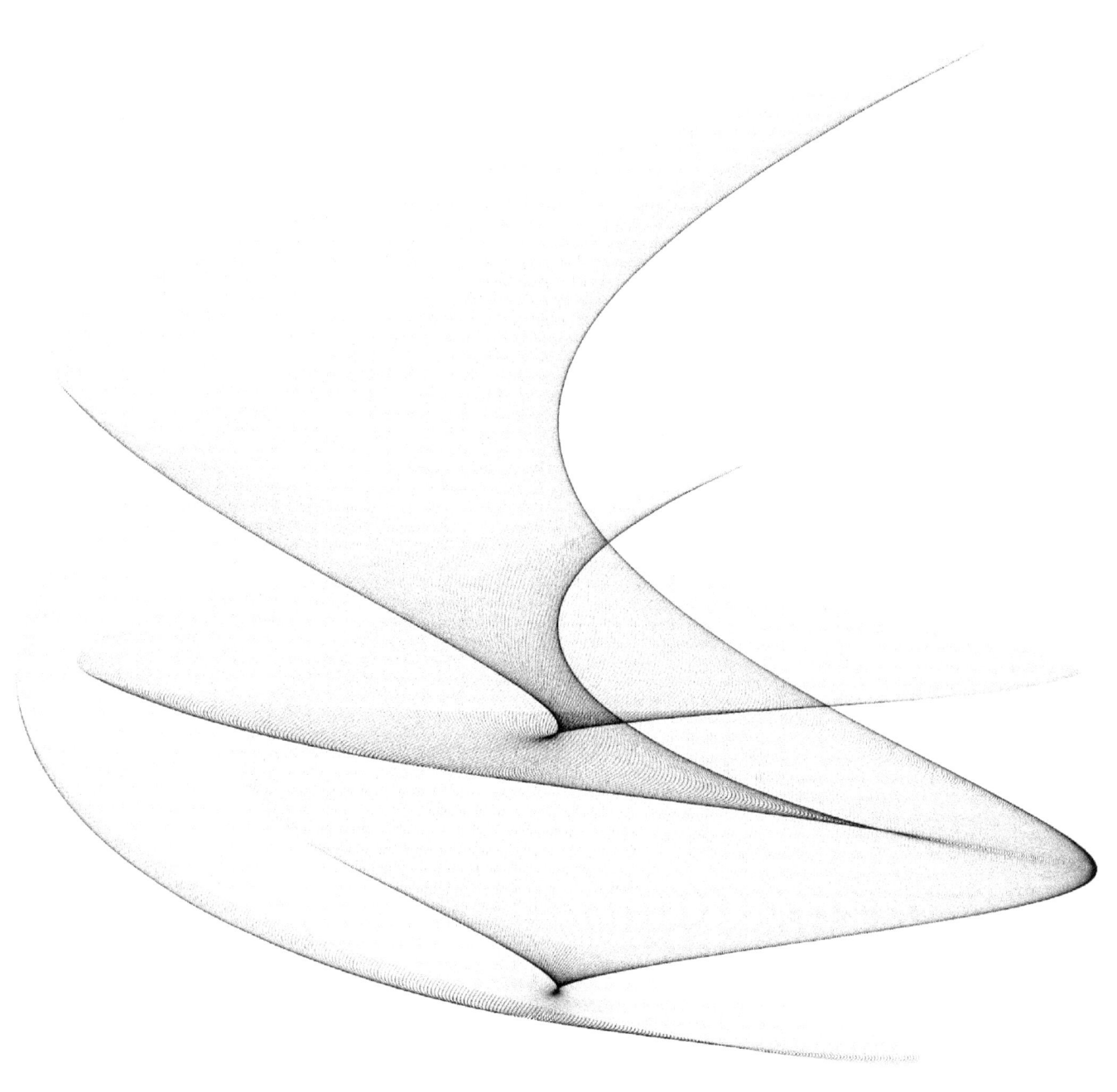

Don't belittle yourself. Be BIG yourself.
Corita Kent

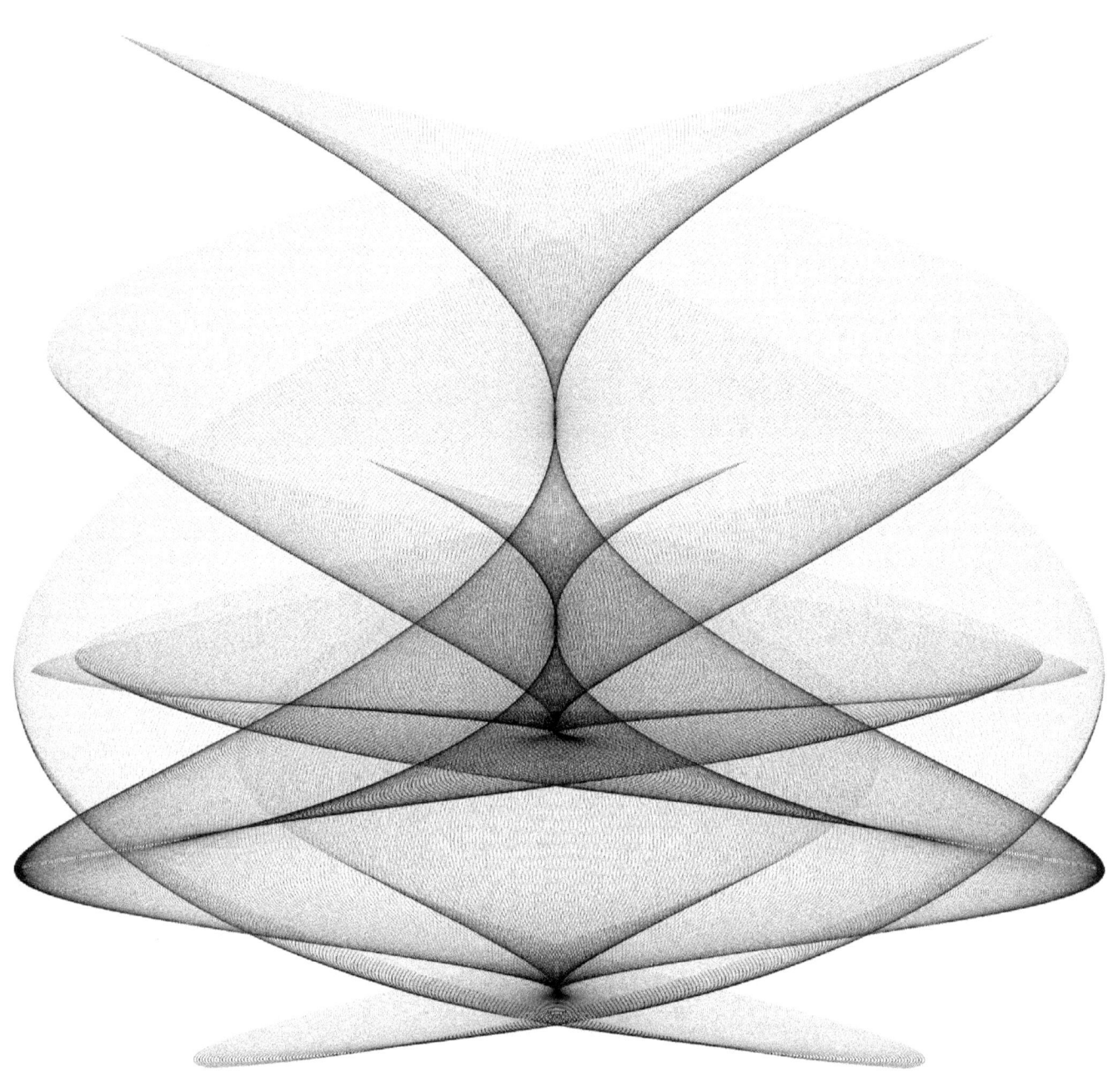

*Peace of mind comes when we
exercise our right to be honest, especially with ourselves.
Jack R. Rose*